Praying to
JESUS
the Messiah

Harry Wendt

**CROSSWAYS
INTERNATIONAL**
Minneapolis, MN

was developed and written by
Harry Wendt, Minneapolis, MN, USA

Illustrations by
Knarelle Beard, Adelaide, South Australia

The Bible text in this publication is from the New Revised Standard Version of the Bible,
copyright 1989 by the Division of Christian Education of the National Council of
Churches of Christ in the United States of America and used by permission.

Praying Like JESUS the Messiah
is published and distributed by
CROSSWAYS INTERNATIONAL
7930 Computer Avenue South
Minneapolis, MN 55435

ISBN 1-891245-15-5

First Edition

Lord, teach us to pray...

There came a day when one of the disciples said to Jesus, "Lord, teach us to pray, as John taught his disciples," Luke 11:1.

Although the Gospels do not suggest that any of the disciples had been a biblical scholar or had studied at the feet of a famous rabbi, they would have known and practiced traditional Jewish prayer life.

Although their everyday language was Aramaic, they would have used **Hebrew** when praying.

They would have prayed **three times each day**, *first* at sunrise, *second* at three o'clock in the afternoon, and *finally* at sundown.

In his writings about prayer and the Lord's Prayer, German scholar Joachim Jeremias points out that within the Jewish community of Jesus' day, *only a hero or a saint could, on rare occasions, make up his own prayer.* The average person recited the prayers designated for use in the community. How then might the disciples have prayed? They would have offered **two prayers**:

 The *Shema Yisrael* (Deuteronomy 6:4,5): "Hear, O Israel: The Lord is our God, the Lord alone. You shall love the Lord your God with all your heart, and with all your soul, and with all you might."

 A series of twelve prayers, or benedictions. By the end of the first century A.D., the list was increased to eighteen. These eighteen benedictions continue to be used in Jewish synagogues today.

What might have prompted the disciples' request? At least one of the disciples (Peter's brother, Andrew; see John 1:35-42) had been associated with John the Baptist. Possibly, Andrew had heard John the Baptist speak about the practice of prayer, and had shared John's teachings with some of the other disciples— including his brother, Peter.

Although the Gospels do not refer to what John taught about prayer, they do report that he told the Pharisees and Sadducees that they were a brood of vipers, that divine wrath was about to overtake them, and that their *genetic* link to Abraham was meaningless before God. What mattered was that they knew and did God's will, Matthew 3:7-10. If John dared say such things to the Jewish religious and political elite, what he taught about prayer would have stressed, "*God* writes the agenda for prayer—*not people.*"

If this happened, it might have prompted the disciples' question, which in expanded form amounted to: "Master, John the Baptist taught his followers to pray in a certain way. If you have suggestions about how you would have us pray, please share them with us," Luke 11:1, 2.

Jesus responded to the disciples' request concerning prayer with, "When you pray, say: *Father.*" Jesus' exhortation to address God as *Father* had, and has, enormous implications.

In the pages that follow, we shall probe the privilege and implications of praying Jesus' way.

Harry Wendt
August 2005

 Note: Many of the illustrations in **Praying Like JESUS the Messiah** make use of a symbol for God. This symbol consists of a circle with four arrows protruding from it. God is *one* (**one** circle), *without beginning or end* (as a *circle*). God always acts in *love* (**arrows**), and that love always goes *out* from God (the arrows point **outward**).

Contents

Unit 1

A BIG GOD—
A BIG STORY

Although the Old Testament contains many examples of
beautiful prayer, in the Psalms in particular, it also contains
prayers which God's people today cannot pray with a good
conscience. Old Testament hopes and dreams must be filtered
through the mind of Jesus the Messiah who established
a kingdom radically different from what the people of His day
were waiting for. What Jesus did with the concept of Holy War
has enormous significance for God's people today.

Our God is a Big God

When asked, "Where do you live?" we usually think of:

■ The name of our street and the number of our house;

■ The name of the city or town in which we live;

■ The state and country in which these are located.

Upper section of **ILLUSTRATION 1A**

This illustration invites us to give more thought to where we really live. Note the underlined words in the following statement made in the mid-nineteenth century by the then president of Harvard University, Dr. Charles Eliot:

> If you say "There is no God," I can only ask how you, <u>a speck of mortal</u> living for <u>a moment of time</u> on <u>an atom of an earth</u> in plain sight of an <u>infinite universe</u> full of incredible <u>beauty</u>, <u>wonder</u> and <u>design</u>, can so confidently hold so improbable a view.

The universe contains tens of billions of galaxies similar to the one depicted in the illustration. Each galaxy contains tens of billions of stars.

The Milky Way galaxy in which we live contains about 100 billion stars. To count these stars at the rate of one per second would take about 3,000 years.

Like billions of other galaxies, the Milky Way galaxy reflects the shape of a giant pinwheel. It spins around its axis once every 200 million years.

If we could travel at the speed of light, it would take about 100,000 years to travel across the Milky Way's diameter—a journey of approximately six trillion miles (9.6 trillion kilometers).

Lower section of **ILLUSTRATION 1A**

This segment depicts the solar system in which Planet Earth is located. *To the left* is the **outer edge of the sun**. Flames, thousands of miles long, leap continually from the sun's surface where the temperature is about 6,000 degrees Centigrade (about 11,000 degrees Fahrenheit).

To the right of the sun are the nine planets within our solar system: **Mercury**, **Venus**, **Earth** (indicated by the **white arrow**), **Mars**, **Jupiter**, **Saturn**, **Uranus**, **Neptune**, and **Pluto**. Although the distances between the planets are obviously not to scale, the relative dimensions of the sun and the planets are.

When compared with other stars and planets, those in our solar system are relatively small. To illustrate: If the sun were placed at the center of Betelgeuse, a bright red star in the constellation Orion, Mercury, Venus, Earth, and Mars would move around the sun as they do at present distances, and remain within Betelgeuse—which is 431 million miles (694 million kilometers) in diameter. Antares, a double and variable star in the constellation Scorpius and the brightest star in the southern sky, is 522 million miles (840 million kilometers) in diameter.

We who know Jesus the Messiah as their forgiving Savior and Servant Lord have a relationship with the God who created this vast universe—and we can address Him as "Father" at any time of the day or night. What a privilege! What a comfort! What an inspiration to praise!

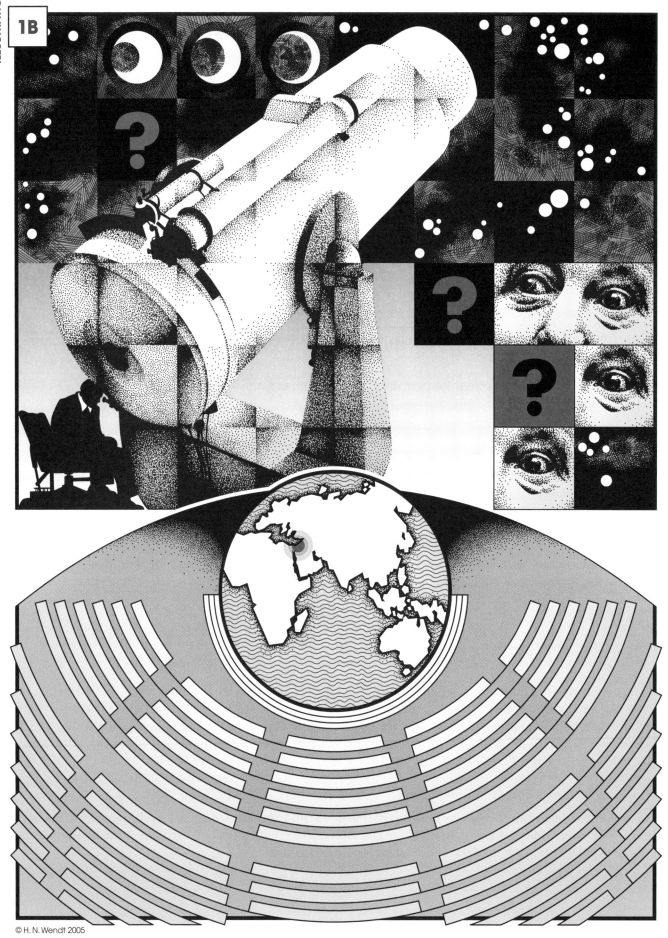

1B

Making Contact with God

Upper section

A person peering (*eyes*) through a *telescope* at a corner of a stylized universe, complete with *phases of the moon* asks:

- Where is God?
- What is God like?
- Can I have any kind of contact with God?

Although things seen through the lens of a telescope point to God's existence and power, they do not reveal God's identity and character.

Lower section

This depicts an *amphitheater*, consisting of a *stage* and *seats*. The scenery on the stage is *Planet Earth*—including the *Middle East* in which the biblical narrative unfolds. The message is:

1. God is not far off among the stars. Although God is there too, God is everywhere. Telescopes and microscopes reveal God's fingerprints *throughout creation*. However, if we wish to know something about God's heart, character, and disposition we must look elsewhere—to God's involvement in *history* as revealed in His *written Word* (the Bible) and *Living Word*, Jesus the Messiah.

2. The Bible teaches that God has made tiny, fragile Planet Earth the special stage for God's activities. God's fingerprints criss-cross all of creation and history. They provide answers to humanity's questions about life, death, life after death, and eternity.

3. Within the illustration, a *bull's-eye* is seen above what we today refer to as the *Middle East*. This corner of Planet Earth was the stage on which the biblical narrative unfolded.

4. The biblical narrative indeed reveals God's *divine drama*. The more we study that drama, the more we learn that we humans do not merely *watch* it happen. We are all on stage, *participating* in it—whether we realize it or not, whether we want to or not.

5. Many have viewed history as meaningless. Shakespeare's Macbeth says:

   > *Life's but a walking shadow, a poor player*
   > *That struts and frets his hour upon the stage*
   > *And then is heard no more: it is a tale*
   > *Told by an idiot, full of sound and fury,*
   > *Signifying nothing.*

6. Those who understand the message revealed in God's written and Living Word must respond: "No, Macbeth! God has revealed His grand plan for humanity—for time and for eternity!" To understand God's grand plan, it is important—even more, *essential*—to understand:

   - The Bible's complex narrative about the rise and fall of kingdoms and empires;
   - How Jesus dealt with the hopes and dreams of God's so-called chosen people.

   To understand these things is to be better equipped to pray Jesus the Messiah's way.

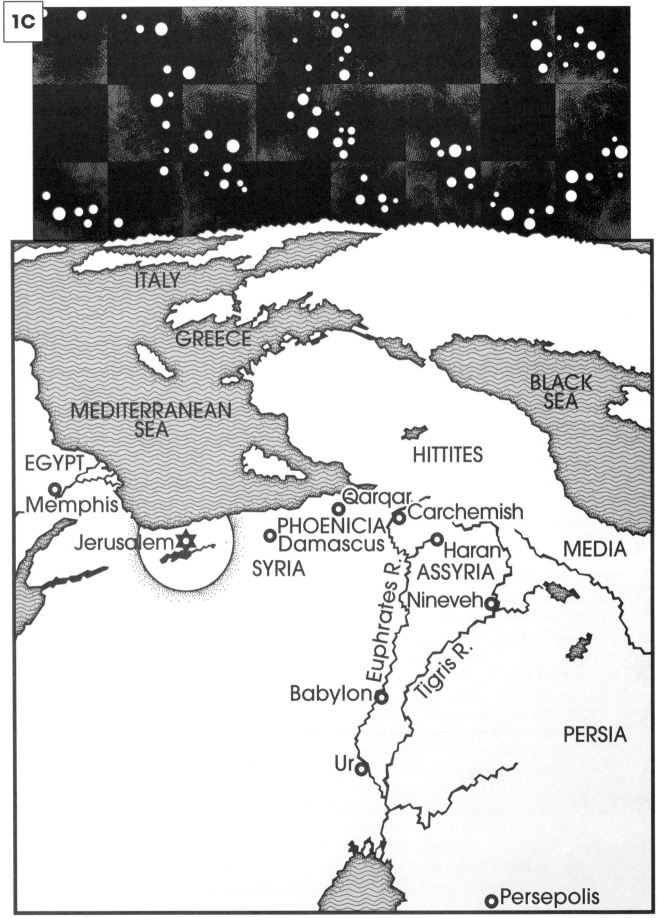

ITALY

GREECE

MEDITERRANEAN
SEA

BLACK
SEA

HITTITES

EGYPT

Memphis

Qarqar

Carchemish

PHOENICIA
Damascus

Haran
ASSYRIA

MEDIA

Jerusalem

SYRIA

Nineveh

Euphrates R.

Tigris R.

Babylon

PERSIA

Ur

Persepolis

The Biblical Stage

ILLUSTRATION 1C provides an "astronaut's view" of the **Mediterranean** stage on which the "rough and tumble" of the biblical narrative unfolds—a narrative that is not about heroes and saints, but about nations, rulers, and people mauling each other to establish their own kingdom and dominion.

Egyptian control: Genesis chs. 37-50 outline how the Israelites came to settle in **EGYPT**. Exodus, Leviticus, Numbers, and Deuteronomy describe:

■ How a pharaoh "who forgot Joseph" eventually enslaved the Israelites, Exodus 1:8;

■ How God rescued His people from Egypt and led them to Mt. Sinai;

■ How God made a covenant with the Israelites at Mt. Sinai;

■ How God sustained them for 40 years, despite their constant murmurs and complaints;

■ How God guided them through the wilderness to the East Bank of the Jordan River.

The land of *Canaan*, the so-called "Promised Land" (**white circle**) is located at center stage. The book of Joshua outlines how the Israelites gained control of it, and divided it among the twelve tribes.

The book of Judges describes the Promised Land being ruled by a series of judges.

Rule by judges gave way to rule by kings—the first of whom were Saul (from Benjamin), David (from Judah), and David's son, Solomon. David captured **Jerusalem** in a rather brutal manner, and made it his capital, 2 Samuel 5:6-10. After Solomon's death, what had been a united kingdom split into the Northern Kingdom (Israel), and the Southern Kingdom (Judah)—never to unite again (see **ILLUSTRATION 1D**).

There were often troubled relations and warfare between the Israelites and **SYRIA**. Good relations prevailed between the Israelites and *Phoenicians*—a sea-faring people whose services the Israelites needed.

The region between the **Tigris** and **Euphrates Rivers** was known as *Mesopotamia*—a name derived from two Greek words meaning "between the rivers."

The *Assyrians* eventually gained control of much of Mesopotamia, including Israel and Judah. They eventually destroyed Israel in 721 B.C., and took tens of thousands of its leading citizens into exile.

The *Babylonians* conquered **ASSYRIA** in 612 B.C., and incorporated its territories (including Judah) into their empire. They crushed revolts in Judah in 597 and 587 B.C. In 587 B.C., they destroyed Jerusalem and the Temple, and took thousands of Judah's leading citizens into exile in Babylon.

The *Persians* conquered *Babylon* in 539 B.C. Although they permitted the Jewish exiles in Babylon to return to their homeland, Judah remained a province of **PERSIA**. Many of the exiles remained in Babylon.

During the period 333-323 B.C., the *Greeks*, under Alexander the Great, overthrew Persia, and established a vast empire—which encompassed Egypt and Judah.

After Alexander's death in 323 B.C., Judah was ruled the Greek *Ptolemies* (based in Egypt) until 198 B.C., when the Greek *Seleucids* (based in **SYRIA**) gained control of it. Although Jewish rulers known as the *Maccabees* and *Hasmoneans* gained independence from Syria in about 160 B.C., some of them ruled in a brutal manner. In 63 B.C. the *Romans* became the controlling power. If we had been among those who experienced life under this succession of foreign powers, what hopes and dreams would we have had?

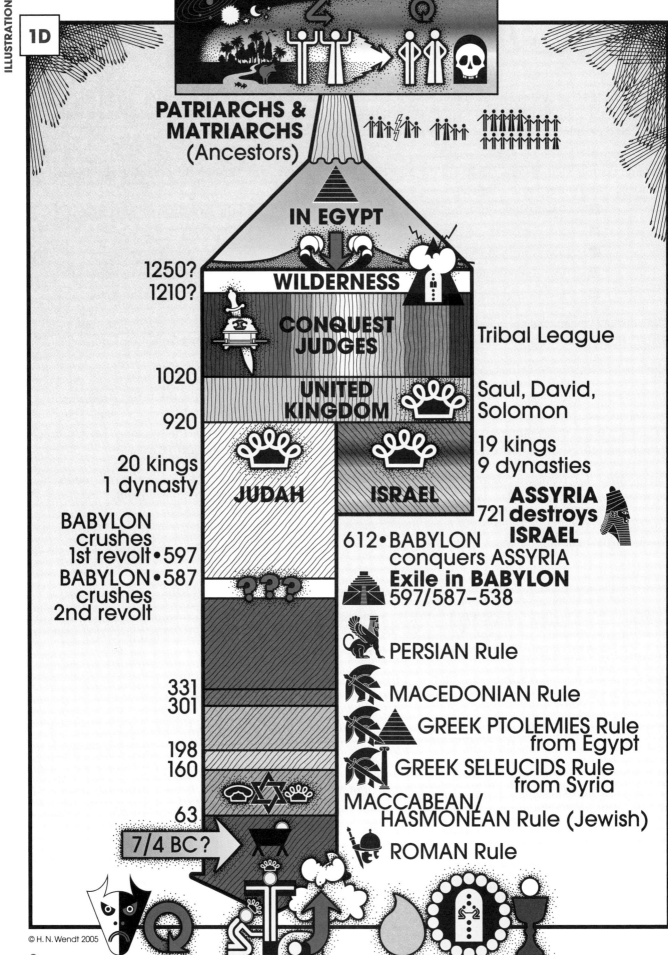

PATRIARCHS & MATRIARCHS (Ancestors)

IN EGYPT

1250?
1210?
WILDERNESS

CONQUEST JUDGES — Tribal League

1020
UNITED KINGDOM — Saul, David, Solomon

920
20 kings 1 dynasty
JUDAH
ISRAEL
19 kings 9 dynasties

ASSYRIA destroys ISRAEL
721

BABYLON crushes 1st revolt • 597
612 • **BABYLON conquers ASSYRIA**

BABYLON • 587 crushes 2nd revolt
Exile in BABYLON 597/587–538

PERSIAN Rule

331
MACEDONIAN Rule
301
GREEK PTOLEMIES Rule from Egypt

198
GREEK SELEUCIDS Rule from Syria
160

MACCABEAN/ HASMONEAN Rule (Jewish)
63

7/4 BC?
ROMAN Rule

8

God's True Kingdom

ILLUSTRATION 1D presents an overview of the Old Testament narrative as outlined in the explanatory notes for **ILLUSTRATION 1C**, and points to the grand finale of that narrative in relation to the breaking in of God's Kingdom through the ministry of Jesus the Messiah (dealt with in greater detail in Unit 2).

1 The *box at the top* of the illustration contains symbols of what God created "in the beginning" (Genesis 1:1-2:25); the first humans and God's will for them; the breaking in of sin and death.

2 *PATRIARCHS & MATRIARCHS:*
- *Abraham, Sarah, Isaac/Hagar, Ishmael*
- *Isaac, Rebekah, Esau, Jacob*
- *Jacob, his two wives and two concubines, his twelve sons and one daughter.*

3 *IN EGYPT:* Genesis 37-50 tell why and how Jacob and his clan (now called the Israelites) moved from Canaan to Egypt (*pyramid*), where they lived for several hundred years.

4 *WILDERNESS:* When a pharaoh "who did not know Joseph" enslaved the Israelites, God rescued them (*arrow passing through open waters*), and led them into the **WILDERNESS** of the Sinai Peninsula where they lived for forty years. After revealing His presence in the form of *cloud and lightning at the top of Mount Sinai* (Exodus 19), God made a *covenant* (Exodus 20:1-21) with the Israelites. This covenant contained *six sections*, the *third* consisting of the *commandments*.

5 *CONQUEST, JUDGES:* God's presence (*Ark of the Covenant*) led the Israelites into Canaan where they engaged in a Holy War (*sword*) in an attempt to rid the land of the Canaanites. They eventually formed a **TRIBAL LEAGUE** and were ruled by leaders referred to as "judges."

6 *UNITED KINGDOM:* Judges were replaced by kings; the first three were *Saul*, *David*, and *Solomon*.

7 *JUDAH/ISRAEL:* After Solomon's death, the kingdom split and never reunited. *ISRAEL* was ruled by *19 kings* from a series of *9 dynasties*; *JUDAH* by a *1 dynasty*—that of David.

8 *Assyria* eventually gained control of Israel and Judah. When Israel revolted, the Assyrians destroyed it and led vast numbers of its citizens into exile. Judah was then ruled by:
- *Assyria* (721-612 B.C.)
- *Babylon* (612–539 B.C.)
- *Persia* (539-332 B.C.)
- The *Macedonians* (Alexander the Great, 332-323 B.C.)
- The *Ptolemies* (Greek rulers in Egypt, 323-198 B.C.)
- The *Seleucids* (Greek rulers in Syria, 198-160 B.C.)
- Judah gained independence under the *Maccabees* and their descendants, the *Hasmoneans* (Jewish, but not from the line of David), 160-63 B.C.
- The *Romans*, who invaded Judah in 63 B.C.

Throughout the postexilic period, many within Judah looked forward to the coming of an "anointed one" who would free them from their enemies and establish the Messianic Age. Eventually, Jesus the Servant-Messiah was born (*manger*). However, Jesus unmasked and conquered the *real enemy, Satan and the power of sin* (*satanic face*, *symbol for sin*), and established the *true kingdom of God*. The symbols depicting the *crowned, crucified, risen, and ascended Servant Jesus; Holy Spirit (dove); new covenant and new commandment; new community; Holy Baptism and Holy Communion* are explained in the units that follow.

The Living Word Interprets

ILLUSTRATION 1E shows how all Old Testament hopes and themes must now be funneled (**funnel**, on which are symbols of the **Servant-King Jesus carrying His cross**, **Jesus' resurrection**, and the **Holy Spirit**) through the mind of Jesus the Messiah—*the Living Word and the Final Interpreter of the Written Word*. Jesus taught and showed His followers what His Father's heart was like, John 14:9 (**symbol for God**).

1 **People:** Our relationship with God is not established by ancestry (i.e., by descent from Abraham, Isaac, and Jacob), but by faith in Jesus as our forgiving Savior and Servant Lord, John 3:1–16.

2 **Land:** The Christian hope centers on life in God's kingdom—wherever that life might be live. It does not focus on life in the land of Canaan, 1 Peter 1:3–5.

3 **Rescue:** Jesus rescues God's people, not from Egypt, Assyria, Babylon, Persia, Greece, or Rome, but from the powers of sin and death, Romans 6:20–23.

4 **Sinai, covenant, law-codes:** In Jesus, God clothed Himself in flesh, John 1:14. Jesus established God's New Covenant with humanity (Mark 14:22–25), and He alone determines what His followers are to believe and how they are to live, Matthew 11:29,30..

5 **False gods:** Swiss theologian John Calvin said that the human mind is an idol factory. Martin Luther said that our "god" is whatever we devote life to. Anything that sidetracks us from living to serve God and others is idolatry, Ephesians 5:5.

6 **Ark of the Covenant, sword:** Jesus alone is the link between heaven and earth, John 1:51. Jesus calls and empowers His own to fight the real enemy: Satan and the demonic powers, Ephesians 6:10–18.

7 **Crown:** Jesus, the final descendant of David, is the eternal King of the universe, Hebrews 1:8.

8 **Jerusalem:** God's people look forward to entering the Eternal Jerusalem, Revelation 21:9–21.

9 **Temple:** God's Temple now consists of "living stones"—people joined by grace through faith to Jesus as Savior and Lord, and in servanthood to each other, 1 Peter 2:5; Ephesians 2:19–22.

10 **Altar of sacrifice:** God wants us to give Him, not dead animals, but our living bodies—to be used throughout life to His glory in the service of others, Romans 12:1.

11 **Lamp** (Wisdom), **scroll:** Jesus is the wisdom of God (1 Corinthians 1:24), and the Word of God, Hebrews 1:1,2. In Jesus, one greater than Solomon has come, Matthew 12:42.

12 **Rule over the nations:** In the latter part of the Old Testament period, some Jews hoped the day would come when they would rule the nations. In Daniel 7:11–4, the "Son of Man" (RSV) is a term for the Jewish people, the "saints of the Most High." However, Jesus is God's "Son of Man," the first of God's new and true people, and Lord of the nations, Ephesians 1:15–23.

13 **Death and the grave:** Jesus has overcome death and the power of the grave, and will one day command the realm of the dead to yield up its dead, John 5:25–29; 1 Corinthians 15.

14 **Praying hands:** Although the Old Testament contains many examples of prayer, Jesus' brothers and sisters look to Him for guidance in prayer, and as the model for prayer.

15 **Funnel, Servant-King Jesus the Messiah, open tomb, dove:** Jesus the Messiah is Lord of Time and Eternity. **Jesus alone determines what Christians are to believe and how they are to live. Jesus is the model for the godly life.** We must direct all our questions to Jesus to obtain God's "final word," God's "final opinion," concerning what we are to believe and how we are to live.

Holy War According to Jesus

The previous illustration referred to a number of events and themes which Jesus the Messiah, God's Living Word, dealt with—*and redefined.* **ILLUSTRATION 1F** focuses on what Jesus did with but *one* of these themes: the concept of Holy War. *Frames 1–4* depict stages in the understanding of Holy War in the Old Testament narrative. Frame 5 depicts the real enemy that Jesus unmasked, and the non-stop spiritual war in which Jesus' brothers and sisters are involved.

1 *Joshua blowing ram's horn; Ark of the Covenant, sword, conquest campaigns:* In events associated with the Exodus from Egypt, the wilderness wanderings, and the conquest under Joshua, God is depicted as a Warrior God who leads the Israelites in Holy Wars against their enemies. Although during and after the conquest, Joshua and the judges led the people into battle, these leaders were but visible agents of Israel's invisible Commander-in Chief, God. (See Deuteronomy 20:10–18; Joshua 3:9–11.)

2 *Crowns, with dagger superimposed; fortress; Ark of the Covenant above location of Jerusalem; arrows denoting David's campaigns to expand the nation's borders:* Holy War remained an active concept during the reigns of Saul, David, Solomon, and the kings of Israel and Judah. Kings waged war to serve national policies and to expand borders. Victory and security depended on military might, fortresses, wealth, human strategies, international treaties, and political scheming rather than on God's power, 2 Samuel chs. 8 and 10.

3 *Symbols for Assyrian king, Babylonian ziggurat, Egyptian pyramid on symbols for God; arrows pointing to Promised Land; roaring lion:* The prophets warned that God would use other nations to fight against His own people, and wreak divine judgment on them, Isaiah 5:26–30; 10:5–11; Jeremiah 5:29–6:9; Amos 3:12–15; Micah 1:10–16. Why? The people had forgotten God's goodness to them, His covenant with them, and His provision for them, Hosea 13:4–6. God would therefore stalk and attack them like a lion, like a leopard, like a bear robbed of her cubs, Hosea 13:7,8.

4 *Jewish zealot with sword; star denoting location of Jerusalem in small postexilic Judah; seven swords pointing out from Judah: During* their time of exile in Babylon, many found hope in the belief that God could and would use a foreign power, Persia, to rescue His people from captivity, and enable them to return to Judah, Isaiah 45:1. *After* the return from Babylon in 538 B.C., Holy War was seen as God's instrument to pour His wrath and vengeance on the nations that had made, and continued to make, life difficult for God's people, Isaiah 61:2; Jeremiah 46:1–51:64; Obadiah 5-14; Nahum 1:2,3; Psalm 137:7–9. A number of Old Testament passages refer to God's people as having seven Gentile enemy nations on their borders, Deuteronomy 7:1; Joshua 3:10; Ezekiel chs. 25–32.

5 *Sword between satanic face in symbol for sin, and Servant-King Jesus with cross:* Jesus revealed humanity's real enemies—Satan, and the power of sin embedded in human nature. Furthermore, He fought and conquered those powers. Jesus equipped, and equips, His people with spiritual discernment to recognize the real enemy, and with spiritual weapons to fight the powers of evil within and around them, 1 Corinthians 14:8; 2 Corinthians 10:3; Ephesians 6:10–18; 1 Timothy 1:18,19. Jesus calls His brothers and sisters to model His servant life in all they think, say, and do, John 13:1–17. The world-wide implications of Jesus' call to servant discipleship are enormous!

UNIT 1 Questions for Reflection

1 **ILLUSTRATION 1A**: Why do many on Planet Earth devote little time to thinking about the fact that they are mere specks of mortals living for a moment of time on an atom of an earth in an infinitely large universe?

2 A variety of views prevail concerning how people enter into a relationship with God. **ILLUSTRATION 1B** depicts two of these:

- *Upper section:* By peering through a telescope or a microscope.
- *Lower section:* By digging into the Bible's "big story."

Which one gets your vote? Why?

3 Why is it important to know something about the geographical stage (**ILLUSTRATION 1C**) on which the biblical narrative unfolds?

4 Familiarize yourself with **ILLUSTRATION 1D** in order to answer the following question:

If the Jewish leaders of Jesus' day were waiting for a messiah who would make Jerusalem his capital city, free them from foreign control, and give them dominion over the world, why would Jesus' ministry have been unacceptable to them?

5 **ILLUSTRATION 1E** depicts a variety of Old Testament themes, and points to the fact that God's New Testament people are to see Jesus the Servant Messiah as the Final Interpreter of those themes.

Explain the significance of each symbol, and how Jesus dealt with what they represent.

6 **ILLUSTRATION 1F** depicts the understanding of Holy War as it unfolds within the sweep of the biblical narrative. The passages listed below relate to the five numbered segments of the illustration. Discuss how God's people are to understand them, and apply them to life today.

a. Joshua 3:9–11; Deuteronomy 20:10–18

b. 2 Samuel chs. 8,10

c. Hosea 13:1–13; Isaiah 10:5–11; Jeremiah chs. 27, 28

d. Joel 3:1–17; Zechariah 14:12–19

e. Ephesians 6:10–18

7 While it is suggested that all the Old Testament Psalms are wonderful models for prayer, what challenges to this view are posed by Psalm 137:7–9?

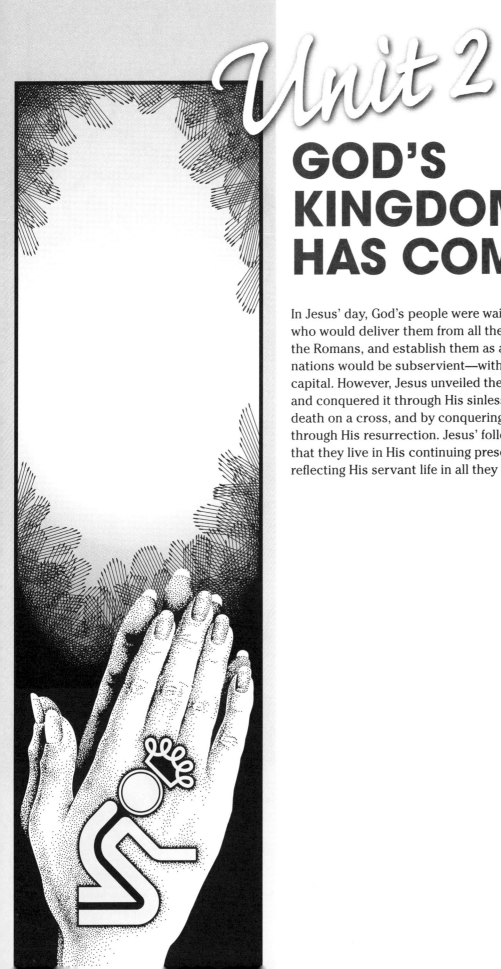

Unit 2

GOD'S KINGDOM HAS COME!

In Jesus' day, God's people were waiting for a human messiah who would deliver them from all their enemies, in particular the Romans, and establish them as a people to whom all other nations would be subservient—with Jerusalem as the world's capital. However, Jesus unveiled the real enemy—the demonic—and conquered it through His sinless servant life and atoning death on a cross, and by conquering the power of the grave through His resurrection. Jesus' followers are to understand that they live in His continuing presence, and are to focus on reflecting His servant life in all they think, say, and do.

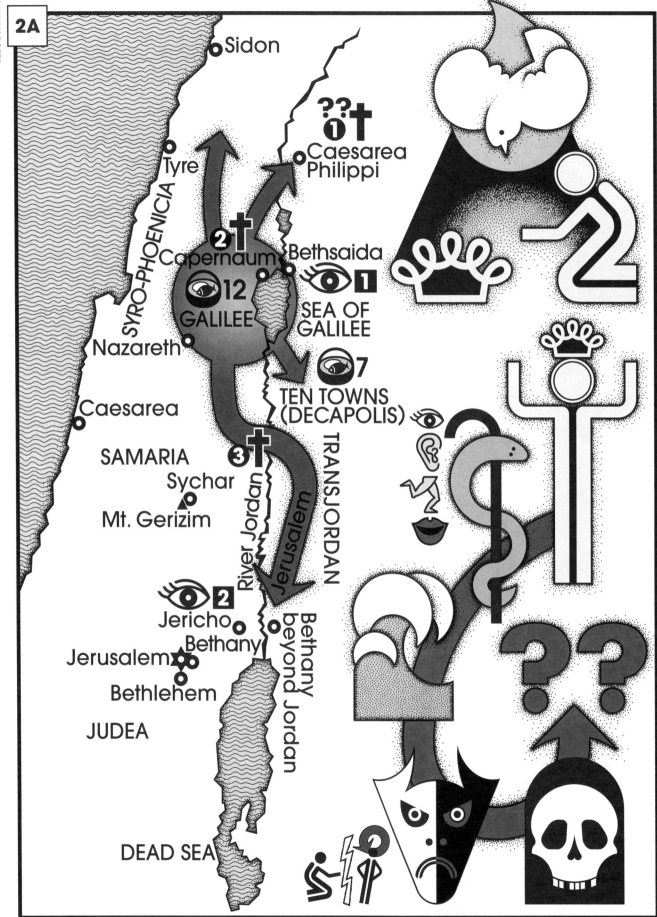

Sidon

Tyre

SYRO-PHOENICIA

??✝
❶✝
Caesarea
Philippi

✝
❷
Capernaum

Bethsaida

👁❶

👁⊙12
GALILEE

SEA OF
GALILEE

👁7

Nazareth

TEN TOWNS
(DECAPOLIS)

Caesarea

SAMARIA

Sychar

✝
❸

River Jordan

Jerusalem

TRANSJORDAN

Mt. Gerizim

👁❷
Jericho

Bethany

Jerusalem

Bethlehem

Bethany
beyond Jordan

JUDEA

DEAD SEA

The Kingdom of God has Come! 2A

In the opening verse of his Gospel, Mark declares the "good news" that Jesus is the Messiah, and that, in His Person and through His ministry, God's true, eternal Kingdom—the Messianic Age—has broken into history.

1 Mark does not include a nativity narrative in his Gospel. In 1:2, he draws on Malachi 3:1 to state that, in Jesus, God will eventually visit the Jerusalem Temple and evaluate its worship system. Mark 1:3 draws on Isaiah 40:3–5 to point out that, in Jesus, God is completing the final rescue, the final "exodus," of His people. However, although Jesus the Messiah comes to rescue God's people and humanity, He does not come to rescue them from any *political* power (such as Rome), but from *the real occupying power, the "deadly trio" of Satan, sin, and death!*

2 When Jesus goes to **Bethany Beyond Jordan** (John 1:28) to be baptized by John the Baptist (***drop of water, dove;*** Mark 1:9–11), the voice from the cloud declares Jesus to be King (***crown**, Psalm 2:7; a Coronation Psalm) and Servant (**servant figure**, Isaiah 42:1; a Servant Song).

3 Immediately after His baptism, Jesus confronts the *real enemy*, **Satan**, Mark 1:12,13. Although Matthew 4:11 and Luke 4:13 state that Satan departed from Jesus after the temptation, Mark makes no mention of Satan leaving Jesus. Instead, Jesus repeatedly confronts the world of the demonic, Mark 1:21–28; 1:32–34; 3:11,12; 3:20–27; 5:1–20; 6:7,13; 7:24–30; 9:14–29 (including its influence among His own disciples, 8:33). In John's Gospel, Jesus declares the Jewish religious leaders to be under demonic control (8:44), and states that, in going to the cross, He will overcome Satan's power and kingdom, 12:31; see also John 13:2; 14:30; 16:11; 17:15.

4 During His ministry, Jesus goes south from **Nazareth** for His baptism (Mark 1:9–11), across the **River Jordan** into the Judean wilderness for His temptation (1:12–13), and then returns to Nazareth, 1:14. He conducts His ministry in **GALILEE** (1:15–7:23), in **SYRO-PHOENICIA** (7:24–30), in the **DECAPOLIS** (7:31–8:13), and then in **Bethsaida**, and as far north as **Caesarea Philippi** (8:13,22,27). When He feeds 5,000 in Galilee with **bread and fish**, there are **12 baskets** of leftovers—one for each tribe in Israel. After feeding 4,000 Gentiles in the Decapolis (8:1–10), there are **7 baskets** of leftovers. (The Jewish people expressed hatred for seven nearby Gentile nations; see Deuteronomy 7:1, Joshua 3:10; Ezekiel chs. 25–32). Jesus enters **Jerusalem** five days before His crucifixion, Mark 11:1.

5 Although Mark states that Jesus *teaches*, he reports less about what Jesus *says* than do Matthew, Luke, and John. However, Jesus' whole *life* proclaims, "I am the Messianic King who walks the way of a Servant." Jesus' life demonstrates the Kingdom He came to establish and the life to which He summons people. Although Jesus Himself does not declare in words that He is God or the Messiah, His actions state that truth. The miracles reported in Mark can be divided into four groups (**ILLUSTRATION 2A**, *lower right*):

   a. ***Miracles over sickness (serpent around staff;*** see Numbers 21:4–9)**:** Jesus gives sight to the *blind* (***eye**, **1**, 8:22–26; **eye**, **2**, 10:46–52); hearing to the *deaf* (***ear***); healthy bodies to the *crippled* (***moving legs***), speech to the *dumb* (***mouth***)—thus fulfilling Isaiah's "signs" (Isaiah 35:5,6).

   b. ***Miracles over nature (white-capped wave):*** Jesus demonstrates the power over the deep ascribed to God in the Old Testament, 4:35–41; 6:45–52; see Psalm 107:23–32.

   c. ***Miracles over demons (satanic face):*** See point 3 above. Jesus commands the demons not to reveal His identity. He needs time to demonstrate the nature of His Messiahship.

   d. ***Miracles over death (tombstone with skull):*** Jesus raised the dead, 5:21–24, 35–43—thus fulfilling the messianic hope expressed in Isaiah 25:8, 26:19, and Daniel 12:1–3.

6 After doing the things outlined in point 5 above, Jesus—on the way north to Caesarea Philippi—asks the disciples *two questions*: "Who do *the people* think I am? Who do *you* think I am?" Peter answers that although the people *do not* see Jesus to be the Messiah, the disciples *do*, Mark 8:27–30. When Jesus predicts His approaching passion three times (❶, *cross,* 8:31–33; ❷, *cross,* 9:30–32; ❸, *cross,* 19:32–34), the disciples are flabbergasted and confused. Prior to Jesus' crucifixion and resurrection, the disciples never clearly understand the nature of Jesus' servant ministry.

7 After Jesus enters the Jerusalem Temple on Palm Sunday (11:1–11), He notes what is taking place within its walls. Jesus returns to the Temple the following day to attack its "sin management system," its "salvation marketing system." The 9,000 priests and Levites serving on the Temple's staff would have been furious with Jesus—and would have wanted Him dead!

8 During the days that followed, Jesus was arrested, tried, and crucified. The irony is that when the religious leaders and political authorities did their worst to Jesus, He did His best for them—and for humanity. Furthermore, when Jesus went to the cross, although Jesus got *crucified*, Satan got *nailed!* Jesus' crucifixion was, after all, His coronation. It was that moment in time when Jesus, the sinless Son of God, carried out the greatest act of servanthood—He gave away His life.

9 After rising from the dead, Jesus returned to Galilee—where He eventually met with the disciples whose eyes had now been opened, Mark 16:1–8; note the word "see" in 16:7.

The Nature of Jesus' Kingdom 2B

1 ILLUSTRATION 2B draws on John 13:1–17 to portray the nature of Jesus' Messiahship. It shows ***Jesus on His knees washing Peter's feet***. (Jews traditionally employed *Gentile slaves* to wash the feet of a guest.) Also included are symbols of Jesus' crucifixion and resurrection (***cross*** and ***open tomb***). None who witnessed Jesus' trial and crucifixion expected Him to return to life. However, Jesus' Father raised Him from the dead and, in so doing, gave **the deciding vote that declared Jesus to be the Messiah!**

2 Around the symbols depicting Jesus' ministry is a ***circle of people holding hands in community***. God's desire is that all live in community, seeking to glorify God and serve each other in all that they do. Unlike most humans, God is not interested in national borders, flags, and skin colors. If anything, God grieves about the ways in which people subdivide the human family.

3 God sends the Holy Spirit (***dove***) to help people understand and embrace the huge truths that relate to Jesus' ministry, and to empower them to live as members of Jesus' servant community.

A verse by George McDonald defines the radical nature of Jesus' kingdom.

> *They were all waiting for a king*
> *to slay their foes and raise them high.*
> *Thou cam'st a little baby thing*
> *that made a woman cry.*

(to which we might add)

> *Thou cam'st to do Thy servant thing,*
> *on cruel cross to die.*

Jesus' <u>One</u> Commandment

Upper section

❶ The Jewish rabbis (teachers) taught that God gave humanity's first parents *two* commandments; they were to serve God and each other. However, Adam and Eve sinned, and eventually God wiped out humanity, preserving only Noah and his three sons (Shem, Ham, and Japheth), and their wives.

❷ According to rabbinic tradition, God gave Noah *seven* commandments. "The commandments of Noah," which were understood to apply to all humanity, were the following: (1) The practice of equity. Prohibitions against: (2) Blaspheming the Name of God, (3) Idolatry, (4) Immorality, (5) Bloodshed, (6) Robbery, (7) Eating an uncooked limb torn from an animal.

❸ After God rescued the Israelites from Egypt in the Exodus, God made a covenant with them at Mt. Sinai. God gave them the Ten Commandments, plus 603 additional commandments. The Ten Commandments are given in Exodus 20:1–17, and repeated in Deuteronomy 5:6–21 with minor variations. The 603 additional commandments are given in Exodus, Leviticus, Numbers, and Deuteronomy. *Judaism insists, and rightly so, that these 613 commandments were given <u>only</u> to the Israelites and their descendants, the Jews.*

❹ After those taken into exile in Babylon in 597 and 587 B.C. began returning to Judah and Jerusalem in 538 B.C., they began developing "oral traditions" to supplement and explain the laws written in the Pentateuch, the first five Old Testament books. Some argued that God had whispered them to Moses, who memorized them and passed them on to Joshua, who passed them on to the elders, who finally passed them on to the members of the postexilic Great Assembly. These oral traditions were finally written down about A.D. 200 in the *Mishnah*. Additional collections of oral traditions were made in writings known as the *Tosefta*, *Gemara*, and *Talmuds*.

❺ Jesus joined *loving God* to *loving neighbor*, Mark 12:28–34.

❻ Still today, Christians debate how the Ten Commandments should be numbered: Four to God and six to neighbor? Or, three to God and seven to neighbor?

❼ Jesus gives His followers only *one* commandment, "Copy Me!" (John 13:1–15,34,35). Jesus the Messiah teaches and models what Christians are to believe *and do*. Any Old Testament commandment repeated in the New Testament is but a commentary on Jesus' one commandment. **Like Jesus, Christians are to use life to glorify God and serve others.**

Lower section

The illustration summarizes how God's children are to serve each other in the spirit of Jesus. It is based on commandments 4–10, as *some* list them. The commandments define our duties to others. God wants us to:

4 establish God-pleasing *parent-child relationships in families*.

5 protect and care for our neighbor's *body*.

6 protect and enrich our neighbor's *marriage*.

7 protect our neighbor's *possessions*.

8 protect our neighbor's *reputation*.

9,10 avoid *coveting*. Here we ask God to protect us from living merely to get and enjoy things, and from manipulating others for our own advantage.

Jesus, Model for the Godly Life 2D

The New Testament teaches that the *Word of God* (*open Bible*, *center*) that created the universe and directs the course of history became incarnate (*in-flesh*) in Jesus (*Servant-King*), John 1:14. God's people now look to Jesus for God's final Word concerning salvation and discipleship. The Christian faith is not *the most important part of life*; it is *life itself*. **Christians are to see all of life as a sacred affair, lived around the presence of Jesus the Messiah. Their one desire is to reflect Jesus in all they do. This desire is to lie at the center of their prayer life.**

1   *Government (**dome**):* Christians take an interest in, and participate in, government so as to enable all to live together harmoniously and happily at local, national, and international levels.

2   *Study (**diplomas**):* Christians develop their minds and abilities to be equipped to serve others in a meaningful, useful way.

3   *Food and drink (**knife, fork, plate**):* Christians eat healthfully in order to live usefully. They eat to live; they do not live to eat. They understand that fast food can cause health problems.

4   *Family life (**parents with children**):* The family is the basic unit of society. Parents influence children enormously—whether they realize it or not. The Christian faith must be taught, shared, modeled, and perpetuated in homes by parents who equip themselves to do so.

5   *The use of money (**dollar sign**):* Money is service in a storable, transferable form. It is not wrong to have money. The question is: How was it obtained, and how is it being used?

6   *Sport and leisure activities (**ball**):* People need to exercise and participate in sporting activities and leisure pursuits in order to keep their bodies and minds healthy and alert.

7   *Work (**factory**):* Christians see daily work as an opportunity to provide needed goods and services for the good of humanity.

8   *The organized church (**church facility**):* According to the New Testament, the term "church" has to do with a community of people—never a building. Nevertheless, Christians gather with other Christians in an "ecclesiastical facility" to worship God together, to help one another grow in faith and discipleship, and to gather others into Jesus' community.

In relation to the above, Jesus' brothers and sisters are to pray:

- for God's guidance to understand the implications of Jesus' ministry for their lives, and
- for God's empowerment to live what they learn.

Questions for Reflection

UNIT 2

1 Those who wish to understand the mind, manner, and mission of Jesus need to have some understanding of the way the Gospel writers present their respective narratives. **ILLUSTRATION 2A** outlines how the first three Gospels (with some variations) portray Jesus' ministry, including His prayer life. Read Mark 1:35, Matthew 14:23.

   a. What *do* they tell us? _____

   b. What do they *not* tell us? _____

2 **ILLUSTRATION 2B** depicts the radical nature of Jesus' Messianic ministry. What do the following passages tell us about what transpired prior to Jesus' arrest, trial, and crucifixion?

   a. Mark 14:10,11, John 13:2. Why did Judas betray Jesus?

   b. John 12:31, 14:30. According to Jesus, who was humanity's "real enemy," and what would Jesus achieve through His crucifixion?

3 **ILLUSTRATION 2C** points to the New Testament's emphasis that Jesus alone is to determine the nature of the discipleship that He wants His brothers and sisters to practice.

   a. What did the exiles taken to Babylon ask God to do on their behalf, Psalm 137 (note vv. 7–9 in particular)?

   b. According to Jesus (Matthew 5:38–42, 26:47–52), what attitude should His brothers and sisters adopt toward those who make life difficult for them?

4 **ILLUSTRATION 2D**: Suggest *prayer goals and thoughts* in relation to living out the spheres of activity denoted by the eight symbols around the Living Word, Jesus the Messiah.

5 The Book of Enoch was written between the times when the Old and New Testaments were written, and reflects Jewish thinking during this period. Among other things, it provides a picture of the final great banquet that will take place when the Messiah comes. The Gentiles will be present and included. But the angel of death will be present, and will use his sword to destroy those Gentiles. The place will run with blood, and the Jewish believers will wade through this blood, and then sit down to dine with the Messiah,(62:1–11).

The Essenes (members of the Qumran community where the Dead Sea scrolls were found) believed that only those Jews who kept the law in the very precise, narrow fashion which the Essenes prescribed would participate in the final Messianic banquet. All Gentiles and Samaritans would be excluded from it. The Essenes wrote, "And then the Messiah of Israel shall come and the chiefs of the clan of Israel shall sit before him, each in the order of his dignity, according to his place in their camp and marches… And no one is going to be allowed in who is smitten in his flesh, or paralyzed in his feet or hands, or lame, or blind, or deaf, or dumb, or smitten in his flesh with a visible blemish." (*The Messianic Rule*, 1QSA, 2:11–22)

   a. In His teaching and actions, what attitude did Jesus display toward these beliefs?

   b. What influence does Jesus want to have on our prayer life, and our day-to-day life?

Unit 3

PRAYER ACCORDING TO JESUS THE MESSIAH

Throughout His life, Jesus conversed with His Father. Jesus continues to assure His forgiven brothers and sisters that they too have joyous access to His heavenly Father. Jesus teaches us that our prayer life is to reflect His own prayer life, and urges us to focus on discerning and fighting the real enemy—and leave it to our heavenly Father to supply our material needs.

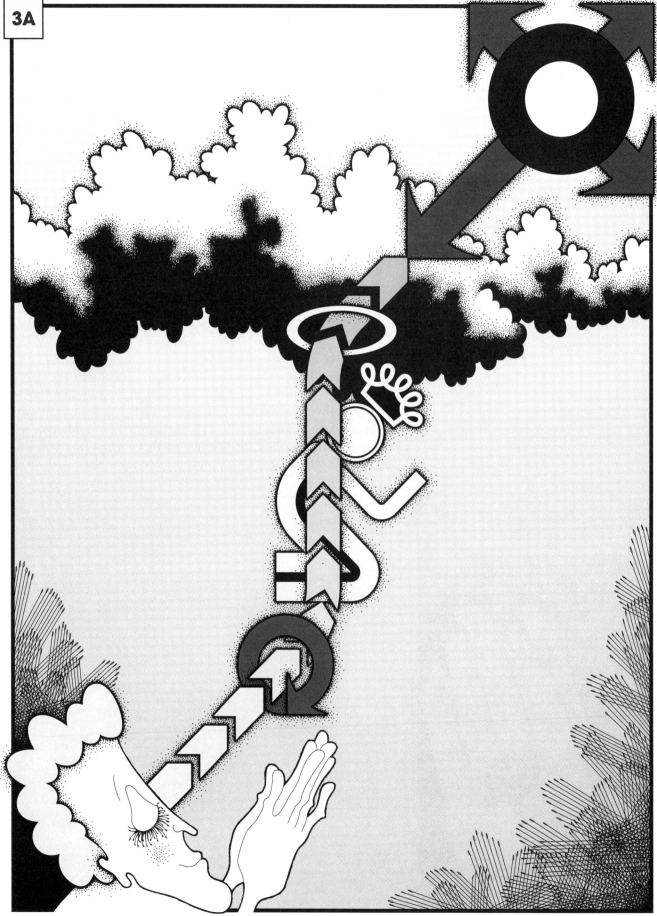

Praying with Confidence

3A

In **ILLUSTRATION 3A**, one of the arrows protruding from the **symbol for God** extends down toward the **person** (let's name him "Sylvester") in the *lower left corner*. Sylvester's **hands are folded in prayer**, and **arrows** (symbolizing praise and prayer) **rise up from him toward God**.

Between God and Sylvester is a depiction of a **Servant-King Jesus**—but with **hands raised in prayer** to denote that Jesus prays for His people, John 17:5–19. Jesus brings His brothers and sisters into the presence of His Father. Note the **symbol for sin beneath Jesus**, and the **halo above Jesus' head**—to depict that God has forgiven and done away with our "sin hat" through the cross of Jesus the Messiah, has given us Jesus' sinless "holy hat" and declared us to be His holy people, His saints.

Our prayer life is to reflect Jesus' prayer life, who, throughout His life, sought only to glorify His Father, and to walk the way of a Servant-without-limit.

The Privilege

 We Christians not only *believe* that God exists, but we also *know* God as a Father and Friend through our relationship with God's Son, our Heavenly Brother, Jesus the Messiah. Although we cannot see God in His incomprehensible majesty, we know what God's heart is like because we have seen it in Jesus the Messiah, John 14:8,9.

 Paul twice says that Christians can pray to the Father as Jesus did, Romans 8:15; Galatians 4:6. On occasion, Jesus prayed "*Abba*, Father," Mark 14:36. In ancient Israel, children used the word *Abba* when addressing their father. The only English word that conveys the true meaning of "Abba, Father" is *daddy*. How wonderful that we may speak with the creator, owner, and preserver of this vast universe and call Him "Our Father, our Daddy" Matthew 6:9.

The Practice

 God loves us, has forgiven us, and seeks an enduring relationship with us, 1 Corinthians 1:2, John 3:16. We may approach God in prayer with confidence, Hebrews 4:16. Jesus gives us *access* into His presence (Romans 5:2; Ephesians 2:18; 3:12) and prays for us, Romans 8:34; Hebrews 9:24; 10:22.

 Prayer is talking *with* God rather than *to* God. If in prayer we merely talk *to* God, the danger is that we use prayer to tell God what *we want for ourselves*, rather than open ourselves to listen to God so that we might learn what *God is like, and what God wants* for us and of us.

 God speaks to us, and teaches us about God's love for us and His will for our lives, through His written Word, the Bible, and His Living Word, Jesus the Messiah. God's children need to *listen to God* by studying and meditating on God's Word, Psalm 119:15,16. Those who *listen to God* in prayerful meditation understand much better what they should *speak to God* about, Colossians 3:17.

 God does not need our prayers; God can survive very well without them. God urges us to pray His way *for our sake*, for God knows that *we need Him*. God's concern is not God's *ego*, but *our welfare*.

Praying in Jesus' Name

Jesus is the *final teacher* about the practice of prayer, and Jesus' example is the divine model of our prayer life.

The Practice

1 In John 16:23; Jesus says to His disciples,

> *If you ask the Father for anything in My name, He will give it to you.* [NEB]

2 Some look on the words *in Jesus' Name* as virtually a mantra, a magic incantation, to extract from God whatever they want for themselves. However, to pray in Jesus' name means to commit ourselves to *learning* what God wants us to believe and to *doing* what God wants us to do.

3 *In Jesus' name* is not a term of *manipulation*, but one of *identification*. When we pray in Jesus' name, we ask that we might use our life as Jesus used life, and that our goals might reflect Jesus' goals.

4 In Philippians 2:5–7, Paul writes:

> *Let the same mind be in you that was in Christ Jesus, who, although He was in the form of God, did not regard equality with God as something to be exploited, but emptied Himself, taking the form of a slave.*

In the *top left corner*, **ILLUSTRATION 3B** depicts the *mind of Jesus the Messiah*. The person in the *lower section* of the illustration prays that God will inspire her to reflect the mind of Jesus more and more in her mind and actions. She prays for guidance and power to use her life as Jesus used His life.

The Promise

1 Jesus promises that prayers *in His name* will be granted, "…He will give it to you," John 16:23. In Matthew 7:7,8 Jesus says:

> *Ask, and it will be given you; search, and you will find; knock, and the door will be opened to you. For everyone who asks receives, everyone who searches finds, and for everyone who knocks, the door will be opened.*

2 God answers *all* prayer. God's answers include: "Yes," "No," "Later," and "Let's do it My way" (and perhaps sometimes, "You've got to be kidding!").

3 If at times we feel our prayers are unanswered, we need to ask, "Did I pray to be empowered to live more *comfortably*, or inspired to live more *usefully*, as a Jesus-like servant?"

4 It is helpful to compare Matthew 7:11 with Luke 11:13. The "good things" referred to in Matthew are interpreted as "the Holy Spirit" in Luke. God always says "Yes!" to people who pray for help to understand Jesus' person and teaching, and for help to pattern their lives on His.

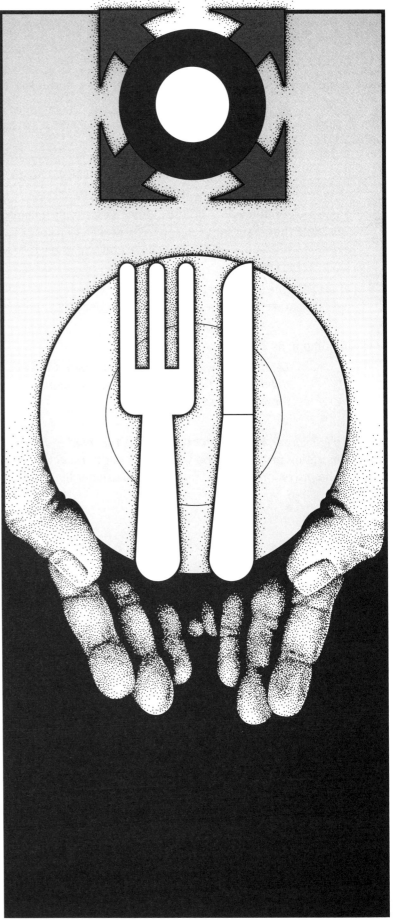

God Our Quartermaster

How do you react to the following story?

> *A young man has completed his military training, and has been posted overseas to a front-line position. As he gets ready to leave his parents and family, his father says to him, "Son, I think you'd better take along some cotton seed. You'll need a little cotton to produce some cloth to make yourself a uniform. And take a few cattle as well. There's nothing like a good barbecued steak once in a while, and you'll need the leather to make yourself some boots. Don't forget to take along a few tools to make yourself a decent gun and some bullets."*

The story is ridiculous. When people go to a battlefront, they go there to fight the enemy—with undivided attention. They do not have time to worry about supplies—and they do not have to. The quartermaster supplies their needs.

Left section

We Christians are constantly at God's *front line* in a full-time battle against Satan. We must study Satan's camouflages and strategies, and equip our minds to fight in Jesus' way by devoting life to serving God and others. We pray for God's guidance, inspiration, and power to reflect Jesus' mind and manner in all we do (***praying hands***, ***Servant-King Jesus***).

Right section

 We are not to worry about supplying our own needs. We do not need to, for God attends to that (*symbol for God;* ***God's hands extended downward, with plate, knife, and fork***). God is our quartermaster. As we look to God for guidance and strength to fight Satan effectively, we also look to God to sustain our physical bodies.

 In Matthew 6:25, Jesus says:

> *Therefore I tell you, do not worry about your life, what you will eat or what you will drink, or about your body, what you will wear. Is not life more than food, and the body more than clothing?*

Jesus argues from the greater to the lesser. If God has provided us with such a precious thing as life, God will provide food to sustain that life. If God has provided us with the miracle of the body in which we reside, God will provide clothing for that body. However, God will provide what *God* knows we need—not what the *advertising world* pressures us to eat and wear. God promises to supply our *needs*—not our *greeds*.

 In Matthew 6:33, Jesus tells us to strive *first* for God's kingdom and righteousness, and to rest assured that as we do that, God will provide our needs. The words "strive *first*" imply: *the one and only concern you are to have in life is…* Luke omits the word *first*, 12:31. In Matthew 4:10, Jesus says we are to worship and serve *only* God. We are to busy ourselves fighting God's battle by using creation and life to serve God and others, and to leave it to God to supply what God knows we need.

 When people have much more than they need, the issue is not that God has singled them out for special blessing. Rather, they have merely been entrusted with much to share with those who have little. Although God has *provided* for humanity's needs, humanity has not *divided* justly what God supplies!

Questions for Reflection

1 Keep in mind the message of **ILLUSTRATION 3A**, as you discuss the following statements:

a. "It would be great to talk with God in prayer, but He seems so far away, and I don't really know what He is like."

_____

b. "I really have no right to pray to God. I am so sinful and unworthy."

_____

c. "I am so glad that I can talk to God in prayer. There are so many things that I feel I must tell Him."

_____

d. "I know I should spend more time reading the Bible—but I rarely read it. No matter! I spend a lot of time talking to God in prayer."

_____

2 What message does **ILLUSTRATION 3B** address to the following statements?

a. "Every time I pray, I pray in the name of Jesus. However, for some reason, God does not seem to hear me, or give me what I ask for."

_____

_____

b. "Some of my friends tell me that they prayed to God to bless them with affluence—and He gave them what they asked for. Sometimes, I also pray for affluence—but for some reason God does not give it to me. My friends suggest the reason why is that my faith is not strong enough, and that I should pray more fervently."

_____

_____

3 According to Jesus and the New Testament writers, Christians are to see themselves as being on the "front line" of a non-stop spiritual battle—throughout life, Ephesians 6:10–14. Put **ILLUSTRATION 3C** to work to deal with the following questions.

a. What should Christians focus on in their prayer life?

_____

d. Why do they not need to look on prayer as presenting God with a daily shopping list in relation to what they wear, eat, and drink?

_____

c. What negative influence can the advertising world have on a person's prayer agenda?

_____

d. Some see prayer as a "Blab it and grab it" procedure. What does this mean? Why is it misguided?

_____

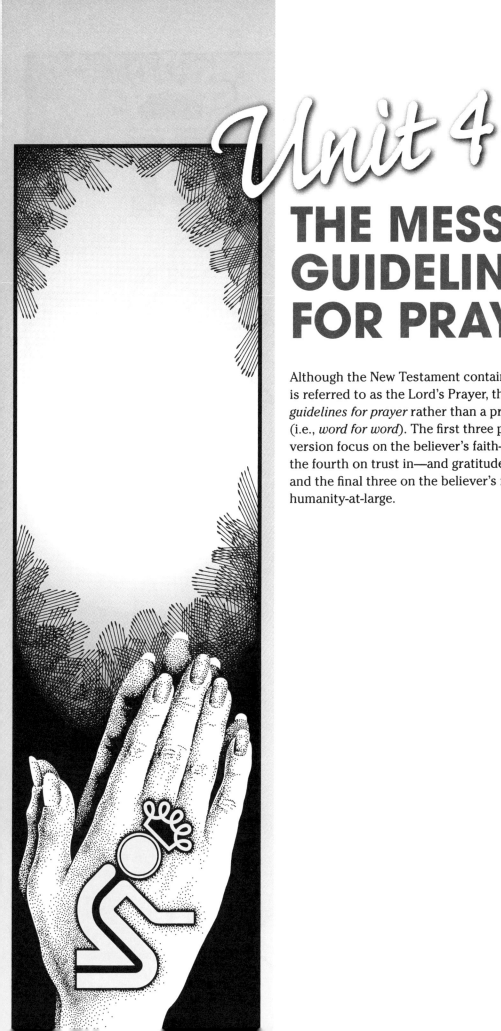

Unit 4
THE MESSIAH'S GUIDELINES FOR PRAYER

Although the New Testament contains two examples of what is referred to as the Lord's Prayer, these examples constitute *guidelines for prayer* rather than a prayer to be offered *verbatim* (i.e., *word for word*). The first three petitions of Matthew's version focus on the believer's faith-walk in relation to God, the fourth on trust in—and gratitude to—God as provider, and the final three on the believer's faith-walk in relation to humanity-at-large.

4A

POWER
POSITION
PROFIT
PLEASURE

34

The Christian's Spiritual War 4A

ILLUSTRATION 4A depicts the two realms or kingdoms that seek to control our lives.

Upper section

The Kingdom of God

Our citizenship in God's Kingdom is brought about by Jesus the Messiah (*left segment, **glorified Jesus the Messiah with hands raised***). Jesus works through His Holy Spirit (***dove***) who in turn uses God's Word and sacraments (***Bible, symbols for Holy Baptism and the Lord's Supper***) to bring us to saving faith in Jesus as forgiving Savior and Servant Lord, and so to membership in God's eternal family. **The entry point in God's Kingdom is Jesus' redeeming cross and victory over death** (***arrow** pointing from left segment to right segment; **cross and open tomb***).

The Kingdom of God does not have geographical borders. It consists of people who live in faith and obedience under God as King (*right segment, **symbol for God, crown, servant figure***). These people serve God and others in thought, word, and deed.

Lower section

The Kingdom of the Devil, the World, and our Flesh

- The Bible, in particular the New Testament, frequently refers to Satan, 1 Chronicles 21:1; Matthew 4:1–11; 1 Peter 5:8,9; Revelation 12:9 (*left segment, **satanic face***). *The demonic is every spirit, person, power, institution, and pressure that would sidetrack us from living to serve God and others into living to serve ourselves.*

- Satan works through the *world order* (***Planet Earth with words superimposed***) and the *sinful human heart* (***symbol for sin on law-codes in human heart***) to persuade people to live for themselves—which is really for Satan. Satan suggests all that matters is ***POWER** for self*, ***POSITION** for self*, ***PROFIT** for self*, and ***PLEASURE** for self*.

- Those who live under Satan reject God as King of their lives, and adopt an indifferent or arrogant attitude toward God (*right segment, **crown and symbols for God canceled out; person in posture of indifference beneath symbol for sin***).

- Note the ***arrow*** at the bottom of this section pointing from the *left segment to the right segment*. In the *left segment* are symbols of the "deadly trio" (*Satan, world order, sinful human heart*). In the *right segment* are symbols of the influence the deadly trio want to have on human life. Satan is quite happy to have people live *decent* lives as the world understands *decency*—as long as they think their "good deeds" make them acceptable to God.

Both kingdoms depicted in **ILLUSTRATION 4A** struggle for control of the lives of Christians. **The Kingdom of God is present *imperfectly* in Christians in this life; it will be present *perfectly* only in heaven.**

The Lord's Prayer
The Christian's War Cry

BACKGROUND

In Jesus' day, and during the first centuries of the Christian era, the Gentiles (non-Jews) used long introductions when they addressed their gods and their rulers. When doing so, they took care to make sure they got all the titles correct, lest the god (often identified with their political ruler, e.g., Caesar) get upset. Names and titles mattered.

The early church historian, Eusebius, reports that when, in about A.D. 300, Galerius Caesar issued a decree to ease the persecution of Christians, the opening section read as follows:

> *The Emperor Caesar, Galerius, Valerius, Maximanus, Invictus, Augustus, Pontifex Maximus, Germanicus Maximus, Egypticus Maximus, Phoebicus Maximus, Sarmenticus Maximus (five times), Persecus Maximus (twice), Carpicus Maximus (six times), Armenicus Maximus, Medicus Maximus, Abendicu Maximus, Holder of Tribunical Authority for the 20th time, Emperor for the 19th, consul for the 8th, Pater Patriae Pro-Consul.*

In Exodus 4:22, God refers to His people, the Israelites, as "His son"; see also Hosea 11:1. Elsewhere in the Old Testament, especially in the latter chapters of Isaiah, the term is used in an adjectival manner to describe God's feelings toward His people. However, *the word "Father" was never used <u>by people</u> in direct address to God.*

There is reason to believe that *Jesus was the first person to address God in this way.*

Although Jesus and the disciples spoke *Aramaic*, the New Testament writings are in *Greek*. However, there are traces of Aramaic within those Greek writings. For example, when Jesus prayed in the Garden of Gethsemane on the night before His crucifixion (Mark 14:36), He began with the words, "*Abba*, Father." Each time *Abba* is used in the New Testament (Mark 14:36, Romans 8:15, Galatians 4:6), the Greek word for "Father" immediately follows.

In Jesus' day, *Abba* was the Aramaic word that children would use when addressing their father. Still today in some parts of the Middle East, the first word that children learn is *Abba*. The "a" at the end is the definite article. *Abba* really means "the father." But "*the* father" can also mean "*my* father," or "*our* father." This Aramaic term became the defining word for the new relationship that believers have with God through Jesus the Messiah.

When we recall the linking of the words *Abba, Father* in Mark 14:36, Romans 8:15, and Galatians 4:6, and the use of the Aramaic language by Jesus and the disciples, we can conclude that Jesus endorsed the use of *everyday language* in praying to God. Prayers do not have to be offered in any *specific language*, such as Hebrew or, say, Latin. And just as children could talk to their father at any time of the day or night, members of God's family can talk to their heavenly Father at any time of the day or night.

The significance of the new relationship expressed by the word "Father" was reflected in worship practices in the early Christian community. Churches were built in two sections, one section for believers, and another section for catechumens—people receiving instruction, but who had not as yet professed faith in Jesus and been baptized into His family. The catechumens were permitted to listen to the sermon and instruction sessions, but were then politely ushered out of the building. Those who had completed their course of instruction, expressed faith in Jesus, and been baptized, would remain and celebrate Holy Communion. It was considered inappropriate for those not yet baptized to take part in this sacred meal.

Furthermore, the Lord's Prayer was never recited with anyone except the baptized. Joachim Jeremias suggests that the reason for this practice was that because *Abba* is the first word in that prayer, those who had not yet come to faith in Jesus were not able to address God in the Spirit as "Daddy." They did not as yet have the kind of relationship with God established only through faith in Jesus the Messiah as forgiving Savior and servant Lord.

THE LORD'S PRAYER IN THE NEW TESTAMENT

■ Two Gospels tell of the origin of the Lord's Prayer, Matthew 6:9–13, Luke 11:1–4. In Matthew, Jesus gives it as a pattern for prayer rather than as words to be repeated verbatim ("Pray then *like this*," 6:9). In giving His prayer, Jesus urges the disciples to avoid display, wordiness, and pointless requests in their prayer life. In Luke, Jesus gives the prayer as His guideline for prayer when the disciples ask Jesus to teach them to pray, as John had taught his disciples, 11:1,2.

■ Some suggest that while the first three and the last three petitions ask for *spiritual* things, the fourth petition ("Give us this day our daily bread") asks for *material* things. However, all petitions ask for *Spirit*-ual things, namely, that God the Holy Spirit might empower us to reflect Jesus' attitudes and actions in all we think, say, and do. We pray that our lives will demonstrate Jesus' attitude towards His Father, the created order, and other people.

■ **In the Lord's Prayer, we do not *instruct God*, but rather we ask God to *instruct us*. We do not pray to *inform God*, but we pray that God might *reform us*. We ask God to teach and empower us to serve God and others—in the spirit of Jesus the Messiah, our forgiving Savior and Servant Lord.**

■ Each petition uses few words to express profound truths about what God wants to happen in *our lives*, and how God wants to use us to influence *the lives of others*.

THE CONTENTS OF THE LORD'S PRAYER

The traditional version of the Lord's Prayer is:

> *Our Father, who art in heaven,*
> *Hallowed be Thy name;*
> *Thy kingdom come,*
> *Thy will be done,*
>   *on earth as it is in heaven.*
> *Give us this day our daily bread;*
> *And forgive us our trespasses,*
>   *as we forgive those who trespass against us;*
> *Lead us not into temptation,*
> *But deliver us from evil.*
>   *For Thine is the kingdom, and the power, and the glory forever and ever.*
> *Amen.*

In what follows, the wording is from the NRSV translation of Matthew 6:9–13.

INTRODUCTION: *Our Father in Heaven*

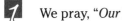 We pray, "*Our* Father"—not, "*My* Father." We bring before God the needs of *all* people, as well as our own, 1 John 3:14–18.

 We approach God with confidence as "Our *Father*," rejoicing in the fact that God, the Sustainer of all, wants only what is best for us, Psalm 100.

 We pray with trust "*in heaven*," not to suggest that God is *distant*, but to confess that God is *different* from earthly fathers. God's power and wisdom know no limits, and God's loving concern for our welfare never varies, Psalm 103:1–5.

PETITION 1: *Hallowed be Your name*

 To *hallow* is to treat as holy, to respect and hold in awe, to revere a person as that person deserves to

be treated. In this petition, *name* does not refer to one of God's titles or *name tags*, but to God as God is, Leviticus 24:16; John 17:6.

 In the first petition we pray that, through His *written Word* (the Bible) and *Living Word* (Jesus the Messiah), God will:

    a. Teach us to know God as maker, owner, sustainer, and Lord of creation, and to give God the respect, gratitude, and obedience due to Him.

    b. Enlighten us to detect and reject every satanic lie.

    c. Use us to influence others to hallow and honor God.

PETITION 2: *Your kingdom come*

 If God's Kingdom prevailed everywhere on earth, there would be no point in praying these words. However, on earth the kingdom of the *deadly trio* holds many in its power.

 We pray that, through His written and Living Word, God might enlighten us—and others through us—to understand the nature of the two kingdoms, to flee Satan's kingdom, and submit to God's Kingdom. Furthermore, we commit ourselves to work toward drawing other people into God's Kingdom.

PETITION 3: *Your will be done*

 We ask God to help us, through His written and living Word, to know and distinguish between *God's will*, and the will of the deadly trio.

 We ask God to equip us—and others through us—to know and submit to God's will for our lives.

 We also commit ourselves to work toward helping others know and do God's will.

REFRAIN: *on earth as it is in heaven*

 These words apply to each of the first three petitions, whose messages then are:

    Hallowed be Your Name *on earth as it is in heaven.*
    Your kingdom come *on earth as it is in heaven.*
    Your will be done *on earth as it is in heaven.*

 These words remind us that where God is in complete control ("in heaven"), all is well. There God's name is hallowed, God's kingdom prevails, and God's will is done. However, "on earth" the deadly trio of Satan, the world order, and sinful flesh (corrupt human nature) strive to mislead humanity. (**ILLUSTRATION 4A** depicts the two realms, the struggle between them, and the goal that each seeks.) We pray, then, that things *on earth* may become increasingly more as they are *in heaven.*

PETITION 4: *Give us this day our daily bread*

 The term *daily bread* means all we need each day to sustain and support life.

 God gives (*supplies*) our daily bread (*needs*) whether we ask or not, and whether we thank God or not. God will continue to do so.

 In the fourth petition, we ask God to give us awareness and gratitude: *awareness* of the origin of *our* daily bread, and *gratitude* to the Giver (supplier). God supplies our needs as a by-product of our daily work, which God also provides and empowers.

 Because God assures us that God is the *quartermaster* (**ILLUSTRATION 3C**) who supplies our needs, our trust in God frees us from unnecessary earthly concerns. We can devote ourselves to the service of others—and therefore to the service of God!

 In praying *us* and *our*—rather than *me* and *my*—we commit ourselves to be God's instruments to supply the needs of all who live on this global village called Planet Earth.

PETITION 5: *Forgive us our debts, as we also have forgiven our debtors*

1 It is important for God's people to understand that the original Greek text states: "Forgive us our debts, as we also *have forgiven* our debtors." The term "debts" points to the fact that we have failed to serve others as we should have. We are in debt to them in that we owe them acts of loving service. The petition stresses that we are to forgive *others* their sins and failures *before* we ask God to forgive us *our* sins and failures. Those who refuse to forgive others forfeit the right to claim God's forgiveness for themselves, Matthew 18:23–35. That others sin against us is the *first sin*. To refuse to forgive them is the *second sin*, which in turn leads to the *third sin*—the failure to serve them.

2 In Jesus, God has already forgiven us. God has removed our sins as far from us as east is from west, Psalm 103:12. God's goal is now to help us become more what God wants us to be—like Jesus. Our motivation for obedience is our gratitude to God for His forgiving grace and providing care.

3 Similarly, we are to forgive others the wrong they do to us, and devote ourselves to helping them become what *God* wants them to be—not what *they* want to be!

PETITION 6: *Lead us not into temptation*

1 God tempts no one to sin, James 1:13–15. However, God permits us to encounter many situations and difficulties designed to strengthen our spiritual muscles and keep them strong. For example, when sickness and adversity strike others, God gives us an opportunity to be a *little Jesus* to the hurting and helpless. When sickness and adversity strike us, God gives us an opportunity to be the *helpless, suffering Jesus* whom others can serve, Matthew 25:31–40.

2 In this petition, we pray that God will help us deal with every situation in life in a way that is in keeping with God's will for us. We pray that, in our attitudes and actions, God might help us reflect the mind of Jesus in every situation, and use us to help others do the same.

PETITION 7: *But deliver us from evil*
better: *But rescue us from the Evil One*

1 The Greek text of this passage (Matthew 6:13) permits either translation. The first views evil broadly, and may be construed as merely undesirable experiences. The second asks for deliverance from Satan's realm at work in the world. On the basis of Jesus' ministry, there is good reason to believe that the second translation expresses what Jesus intended.

2 If the second translation is accepted, the sixth and seventh petitions form a unit that says, "In the tests that come to us throughout life, help us to know and do God's will, and deliver us from Satan's temptations to do his will."

3 "Deliver us from the Evil One" forms a fitting conclusion to the Lord's Prayer. Jesus looks back over all the noble things He asks us to pray about, and urges us to remember that our walk through life will never be easy. The enemy is around. Although society often treats Satan as a comic-strip character, Jesus exhorts us to view Satan very differently (John 8:44; 1 Peter 5:8,9), and to urge others to do so also.

CONCLUSION: *For Yours is the kingdom, and the power, and the glory, forever and ever. Amen.*

The closing words of the Lord's Prayer ("For Yours is the kingdom, and the power, and the glory, forever and ever") reflect 1 Chronicles 29:11. They are found in *some* ancient New Testament manuscripts. We should understand them as, "For Your is the *kingship*, and the power, and the glory, forever and ever."

Amen is a Hebrew word meaning *truly, truly,* or *certainly, certainly*. It denotes that God gladly hears the kinds of petitions we offer in the Lord's Prayer. Furthermore, God earnestly desires to bring them to pass in our lives—and, through us, in the lives of others.

Questions for Reflection

UNIT 4

1 Study **ILLUSTRATION 4A** carefully, and be ready to explain it to others—including family and friends.

   a. Why is it important that God's people read the Bible regularly and avidly?

   b. How seriously does society-at-large take the concept of the demonic? Why?

   c. How seriously do you take it?

   d. Why is Satan delighted when Christians entrust the work of the church to salaried professional church workers?

2 Members of the Christian community join in praying the Lord's Prayer quite regularly.

   ■ Some pray the Lord's Prayer as though it were a mantra to ensure that they will get whatever they ask for.

   ■ Some see the Lord's Prayer as renewing commitment to a life-long, non-stop mission.

What difference is there in these two approaches?

3 What difference is there between *saying* the Lord's prayer, and *praying* the Lord's Prayer?

4 The opening words of the Lord's Prayer are radical.

   a. What obligation does praying *Our* Father have for those who pray these words?

   b. What joy does praying *Our <u>Father</u>* create in our hearts and lives?

5 When we pray the Lord's Prayer, what are the implications of praying:

   a. The first three petitions?

   b. The fourth petition?

   c. Its final three (some would say *two*) petitions?

40

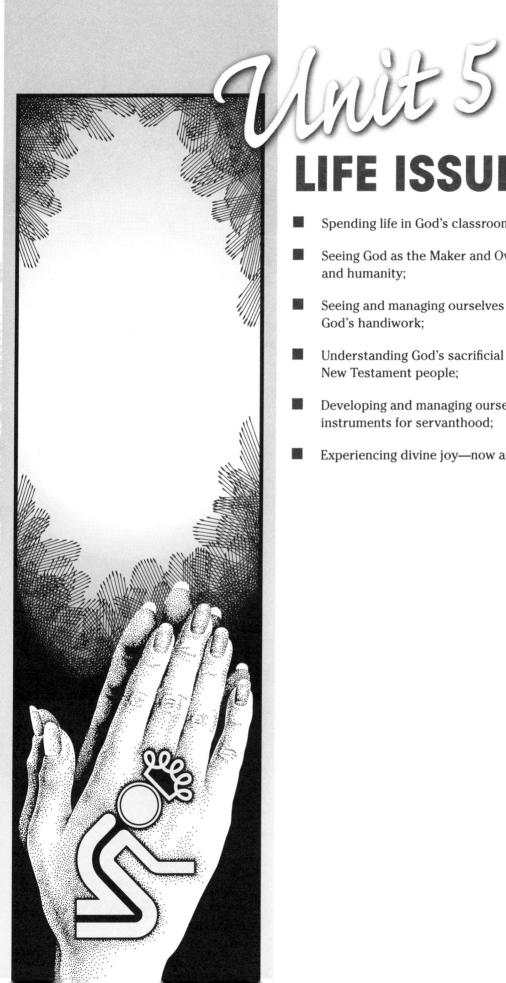

Unit 5
LIFE ISSUES

■ Spending life in God's classroom;

■ Seeing God as the Maker and Owner of creation and humanity;

■ Seeing and managing ourselves as a miracle of God's handiwork;

■ Understanding God's sacrificial system for His New Testament people;

■ Developing and managing ourselves as God's instruments for servanthood;

■ Experiencing divine joy—now and forever.

Copying Jesus the Messiah

Upper section

 Many schoolrooms around the world are equipped with a chalkboard or whiteboard. Sometimes the alphabet is written in perfect script across the top of the board. Students are encouraged to improve their writing skills by studying it, copying it, comparing their efforts with it, and trying to do better next time—to improve their writing skills.

 Peter wrote his first letter to Christians in Asia Minor. Those to whom he wrote were being ridiculed because of their faith in Jesus as forgiving Savior and Servant-Lord, and faced with the constant threat of persecution by the Romans. Peter's goal in writing was to give his readers encouragement and hope, and to help them deal with the challenges that they faced day by day. In doing so, Peter pointed them to Jesus' life as the model for their own life.

> *Christ also suffered for you, leaving you an <u>example</u>, so that you should follow in His steps.*
> (1 Peter 2:21)

The word Peter uses for "example" refers to the perfect line of writing referred to in point 1 above. His appeal is: "Remember that Jesus always did His Father's will, and devoted His life to serving others full-time as His Father wanted them served. At all times, remember that you spend life in Jesus' presence, in Jesus' "classroom." Strive to copy and reflect Jesus in all that you think, say, and do."

Lower section

 The one desire of the Holy Spirit (***dove***) is to make known Jesus' completed, saving work, and to empower people to learn to know Jesus as their forgiving Savior and to follow Him as their servant Lord.

The Holy Spirit makes use of the *written Word* (***Bible***) to point to Jesus, the *Living Word* (***Servant-King Jesus, with basin of water in front of Him and a towel over His arm***; ***crowned Jesus on a cross***; ***open tomb with arrow rising into a cloud***—signifying Jesus' resurrection and ascension). When Jesus washed His disciples' feet (John 13:1–15), He did what no Jew would do. When a guest was welcomed into a house and his feet were washed, the washing was always done by a Gentile slave.

In *Holy Baptism* (***drop of water***), God adopts people into His Eternal Family as Jesus' forgiven brothers and sisters. In the *Lord's Supper* (***bread and cup***), Jesus' brothers and sisters share a meal with Him—a meal in which He gives Himself to them through bread and wine. To participate is to celebrate an eternal link to Jesus, and to His brothers and sisters around the world—and to commit life to serving them without regard for borders, flags, and skin color.

 When Jesus' brothers and sisters pray (***praying hands***), they are to ask for God's guidance and inspiration to live to glorify God (***symbol for God***) by serving others in community—full-time in all they do (***two servant figures in third position on the symbol for covenant, inside large circle of small circles***). They are also to pray at all times to be equipped to discern and overcome the whim and will of the demonic (***cancellation symbol through satanic face and symbol for sin***).

The illustrations that follow point to truths to bear in mind in when praying Jesus' way.

God: Maker and Owner

In Luke 12:16–21, Jesus tells the parable of the Rich Fool. He begins the parable with, "The *land* of a rich man produced abundantly." The land produced, not the man—and God owns the universe, Planet Earth, and all land.

Eventually God said to the Rich Fool, "You fool! This very night your life is being *demanded* of you." The term "demanded" has to do with the repayment of a loan. The rich man had been acting as though he "owned" both "his" land and what it produced, and "his" body and life. God responded, "Wrong both times! I own all land, and I have been lending you the body in which life resides. Today I plan to take back the life I have been lending you."

ILLUSTRATION 5B depicts the biblical truths underlying God's response to the Rich Fool. It shows ***Planet Earth*** and a ***human being***, with ***God's ownership label*** attached to each.

Upper section

 God made and owns the universe, including Planet Earth. Everything belongs to God. We humans create and own nothing. We merely use what belongs to God, and are to do so responsibly.

 There is no such thing as "Christian *giving*." People cannot give what they do not own. God's people are to see themselves as called, not to *give more*, but to *rob less*. They are to practice Christian *managing*, *caring*, and *sharing* in all they do.

Lower Section

 God made and owns *all people* on Planet Earth.

 God has endowed us with faculties and abilities. We are to view these with respect, develop them responsibly and wisely, and use them to glorify God by serving others.

3 Our actions toward others are to reflect God's prior actions toward us, 1 John 4:19–21. We do not love others so that God may love us; we love others to reflect the wonderful truth that God already loves us.

4 When we live according to God's will reflected in the life of Jesus the Messiah, we find meaning and joy in life, and bring meaning and joy to others.

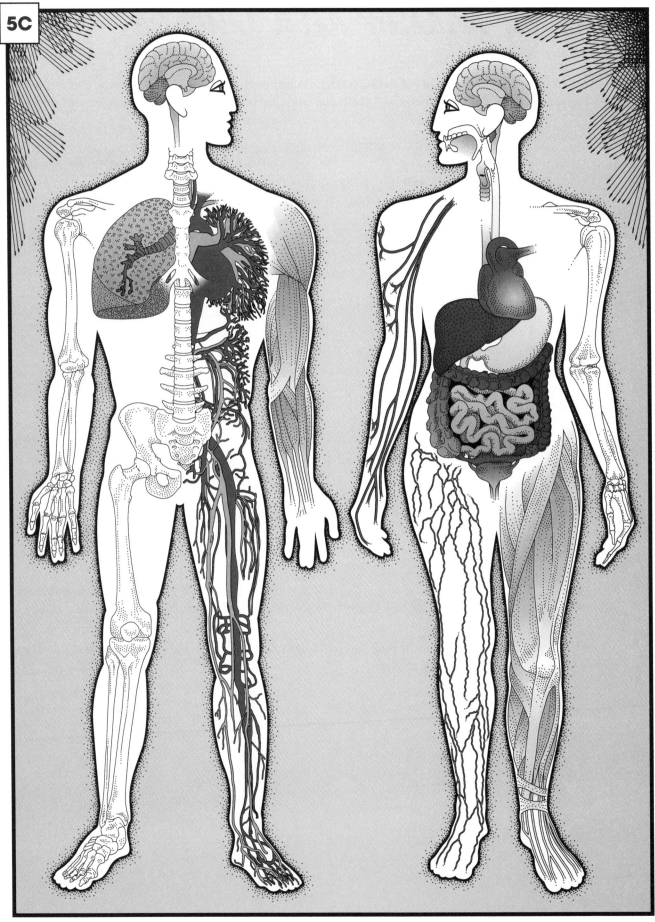

The Wonder That We Are

5C

ILLUSTRATION 1A and **ILLUSTRATION 1B** remind us that when we look at the heavens through a telescope, we see a vast universe. **ILLUSTRATION 5C**, which depicts a male and a female body, helps us understand that when we study the human body through a microscope, we see another incredible universe.

1 If we could join end-to-end all the *veins*, *arteries*, and *capillaries* found in the average human body, they would reach from two to four times around the equator—or 60,000 to 100,000 miles (97,000 to 160,000 km).

2 The body houses the most amazing pumping device in the world—the human *heart*. Its average output is about 72 pumping actions per minute, 100,000 per day, 35 million per year, and 2.5 billion in the average lifetime.

3 The human *eye* has about 130 million light receptors and about seven million sensory terminals for sight. Each eye has about 300,000 "lines" going to the brain. Although the eye transmits pictures to the brain upside down, the brain perceives them right side up.

4 The human ear is the most amazing musical instrument in the world. When we strike a chord on the piano, we think the piano makes a sound. It does not. It merely makes vibrations in the air. The human ear picks these up and interprets them as sound. When we strike two notes next to each other on the piano, the difference in the pitch is obvious. However, the human ear can distinguish about 15 distinct pitches between the two notes. Although a pianist typically has 88 notes to choose from, the human ear can discern about 15,000.

5 In Psalm 139:13,14, we read:

> *It was you who formed my inward parts;*
> *you knit me together in my mother's womb.*
> *I praise you, for I am fearfully and wonderfully made.*

6 Why think about the details outlined in points 1–5 above?

- God made and owns the body in which each of us lives.

- God's will is that we care for the body God is lending us as responsibly as possible, and develop its skills so that we may help others care for "their" body and develop "their" potential skills.

- In our prayer life, God desires that we bear in mind that He made and owns us, that we pray for guidance to develop and use life in a way that reflects the mind and ministry of Jesus the Messiah, our forgiving Savior and Servant Lord, and then help our fellow-tenants on Planet Earth us to do the same.

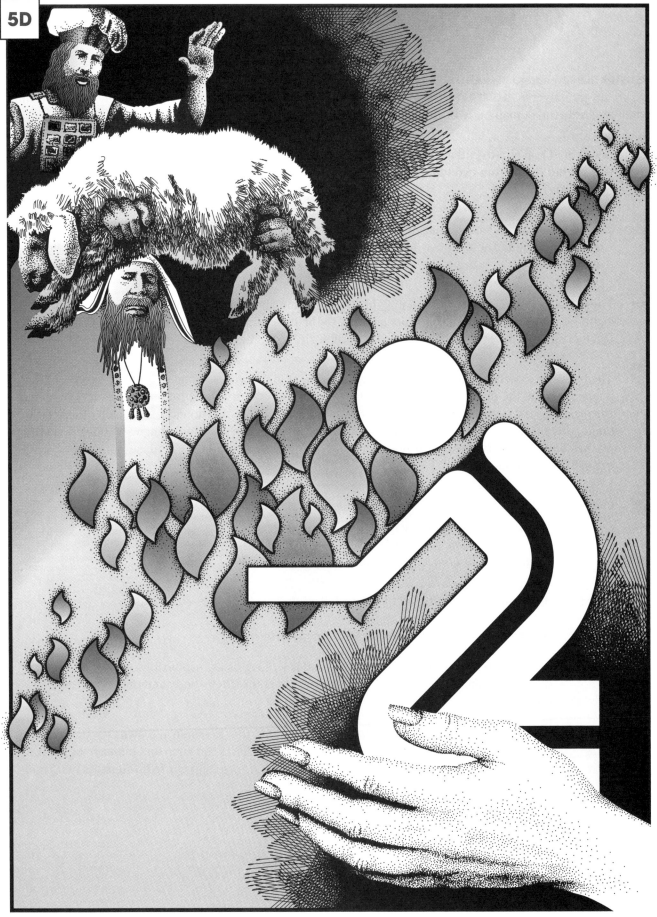

5D

Life as a Fulltime Sacrifice

ILLUSTRATION 5D shows the difference between the *Old Testament sacrificial system* and the *New Testament sacrificial system*.

Upper left section

 In Old Testament times, the Israelites offered a variety of sacrifices, including animal sacrifice (**sheep**) in numerous shrines in Israel. Some of these offerings were ritually burned (**flames**) by the officiating **priests** on an altar at the shrine. There is reason to believe that beyond the time of King Josiah's reform in 621 B.C., sacrifices could be offered *only in the Jerusalem Temple*, 2 Kings chs. 22,23.

 The prophets, who worked prior to the Babylonian destruction of Judah and Jerusalem in 587 B.C., attacked the sacrificial system. They insisted that the sacrificial system was meaningless unless God's people cared for the widow, the orphan, and the needy, Isaiah 1:10–17. Several of the prophets suggest that God had not even commanded the Israelites to offer sacrifices, Amos 5:25; Jeremiah 7:21–23 (RSV and NRSV translations).

Lower right section

 Although Joseph and Mary took Jesus to Jerusalem each year (at least, until He was 12 years of age, Luke 2:41, 42) for the annual Passover observance, we never read of Jesus offering sacrifice during His earthly ministry. Jesus insisted that what mattered was the practice of mercy toward others, not the offering of sacrifice, Hosea 6:6, Matthew 9:13, 12:7.

 The New Testament states that we are to offer our living bodies to God by devoting life, in the spirit of Jesus, to the service of those around us (**servant figure in extended hand**). Paul wrote:

> *I appeal to you, therefore, brothers and sisters, by the mercies of God, to present your bodies as a living sacrifice, holy and acceptable to God, which is your spiritual worship.* (Romans 12:1)

> *Christ died for all, so that those who live might no longer live for themselves, but for Him who died and was raised for them.* (2 Corinthians 5:15)

5E

Preparing Ourselves to Serve

God made us. God owns us. God endows us with abilities. God wants us to care for, and develop, ourselves for use as God's instruments in the service of others. When Jesus engaged in a debate with a lawyer (a teacher of the Jewish Law), the lawyer defined God's will for humanity as follows:

> *You shall love the Lord your God with all your* heart, *and with all your* soul, *and with all your* strength, *and with all your* mind; *and your neighbor as yourself.* (Luke 10:25–27)

Jesus not only *agreed* with him, but told him to *do* these things.

In **ILLUSTRATION 5E**, the segments within the large circle contain symbols designed to help us understand the terms *heart*, *soul*, *strength*, and *mind*. It depicts in yellow a ***person's face and upper body, with arms and fingers extended***. The person is within a ***circle divided into four segments*** representing people's volitional, emotional, physical, and intellectual powers. The illustration incorporates a ***double-headed arrow*** denoting service to God and neighbor, and the ***symbol for sin***—with a ***question mark*** near each. The question marks ask, "Who is directing our walk through life? God (*left*), or the power of sin (*right*)?"

 Heart (*upper left segment*)

The term "heart" refers to our volitional powers. "With all your heart" means "with all your will." God wants us to have an informed will (***law-codes***) equipped to weigh moral issues (***balance*** or ***scales***). As with a ***traffic light***, God wants us to know when not to proceed (***red***), when to proceed with caution (***amber***), and when to proceed with a good conscience (***green***). God's will is that we learn to reflect Jesus' servant life in all that we do (***servant figure on law-codes***).

 Soul (*upper right segment*)

God wants to empower us to develop a Christ-like *demeanor* that attracts others to us, equips us to serve them, and creates unity within our immediate and extended community. Our happy external demeanor (***smiling face-mask***) reflects our inner disposition and helps establish links between us and others, and makes them more willing to listen to any witness that we make to them. An unhappy external demeanor (***unhappy face-mask***) creates barriers between us and others. The ***faces within the segment itself*** reflect a variety of moods and dispositions.

 Strength (*lower right segment*)

The segment contains symbols of ***fruits***, ***cake***, ***candy***, and ***drink***, and a ***person playing tennis***. God wants us to eat and drink healthfully, and to exercise to keep fit. When we do that, our bodies are more likely to be instruments God can use to serve others (***servant figure***), rather than liabilities others must serve. God has also empowered people to provide health care to those in need of it (***serpent around staff***, Numbers 21:4–9).

 Mind (*lower left segment*)

God wants us to study things that will edify us, and equip us to serve others better (***graduation hat***, ***diplomas***, ***books***).

God writes the agenda for our actions. We serve others as *God* wants us to serve them—not as *we* might want to serve them, or as *they* might want to be served. "You shall love your neighbor as yourself" does not mean "50% for others and 50% for me." God wants us to devote life 100% to serving God by serving others.

Our goal is to become more of what God intends us to be, so that we might in turn help others become what God intends them to be.

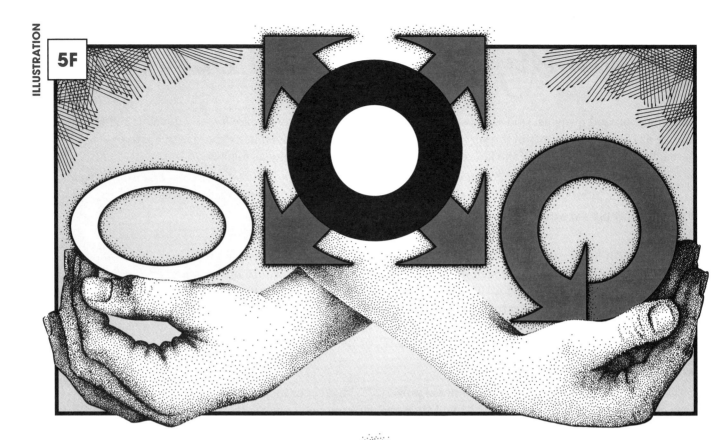

Hearing and Following

5F

Upper section

The upper section of **ILLUSTRATION 5F** shows the *symbol for God, with arms extending from it*. The arms are *crossed over*. In the one to the *left* is a **halo**. In the one to the *right* is the **symbol for sin**. What is the message?

In 2 Corinthians 5:21, Paul speaks of the *great exchange*, the *sweet swap* (to quote a German theologian), that God brought about through Jesus' life, death, and resurrection. Paul says that God took all our sins and put them on Jesus. God then takes all Jesus' achievements and gives them to us. Hence, our sin (**symbol for sin**) is given to Jesus, and Jesus' holiness (**halo**) is given to us. Jesus took humanity's sin to the cross, and suffered the judgment that sin deserves. Jesus won forgiveness for the world. Jesus offers that forgiveness to the world—freely, and without price.

Lower section

For Christians, the outcome of history's Last Day is not in doubt. The decisions relating to that Final Day have already been made—by Jesus.

 Jesus says that when finally He returns in glory, He will command all graves to give up their dead, and gather all nations before Him, John 5:28,29; 1 Corinthians 15:12–28; Matthew 25:31. Jesus will separate humanity into two groups, the **sheep** and the **goats**, Matthew 25:32,33. Jesus will *welcome* (**His arms extended**) the **sheep** and invite them to enter the Eternal Home He has prepared for them. He will *reject the goats*—those who claimed to know Him as forgiving Savior but ignored His call to follow Him as Servant Lord.

 In welcoming the *sheep*, Jesus points out something surprising, but of great importance for God's people. If we ask *people*, "How many people live on Planet Earth?" they will say, "About six billion." If we ask *Jesus* the same question, He will reply, "Two—you and Me. To you, everyone else is Me— in disguise." In Matthew 25:40, Jesus says to those whom He welcomes:

> *Truly, I tell you, just as you did it to one of the least of those who are members of my family, you did it to Me.*

 Jesus links Himself "in disguise" to those who are hungry, thirsty, lonely, lacking clothes, sick, and in prison. Those whom Jesus welcomes and commends express surprise. When they served as they did, they did not do it for the sake of merit or notice, Matthew 25:37–39. *They did it to reflect Jesus' forgiving, caring compassion toward them, and their desire to reflect that forgiving, caring compassion toward others.*

While we wait for our Good Shepherd to give us that final Heavenly Hug, that glorious welcome, into His Eternal Sheepfold—heaven itself—we are to listen to the voice of that Good Shepherd, and let Him direct all our thoughts, words, and actions, John 10:1–18. To understand these things is to possess a treasure-house of insights with regard to:

- The One to Whom we pray;
- What He wants us to pray about;
- How we are to put into practice what we pray about.

1 According to **ILLUSTRATION 5A**:

    a. In what way are we, God's people, to understand ourselves as students spending life in God's classroom? _____

    b. What inspiration can we find in remembering our baptism, and in participating in the Lord's Supper? _____

2 What statements do **ILLUSTRATION 5B**, and the parable of the Rich Fool (Luke 12:16–21), make in terms of guidelines for prayer?

_____

_____

3 **ILLUSTRATION 5C**: The advertising world often encourages people to see the their body as something they are to display to draw attention to themselves.

According to the Bible, what life-long attitude should people adopt toward "their" body?

_____

_____

4 **ILLUSTRATION 5D**: God's Old Testament people saw "sacrifice" in terms of animals, birds, and grain they offered to God in the Jerusalem Temple. According to Jesus (Matthew 9:13, 12:7) and Paul (Romans 12:1):

    a. What are God's people to offer in sacrifice to God? _____

    b. Where are they to offer that sacrifice? _____

    c. How might Jesus be understood as "one greater than the Temple," and "one greater than Solomon," Matthew 12:6–8, 42?

_____

5 **ILLUSTRATION 5E** depicts how people are to understand their "stewardship of self," their "management of self," in terms of how they are to develop and use:

- Their understanding of God's will;
- Their physical powers;
- Their emotional powers;
- Their intellectual powers.

When people learn to understand themselves in relation to heart, soul, strength, and mind, what implication does that understanding have for their prayer life?

_____

_____

6 According to **ILLUSTRATION 5F**:

    a. Why can God's people walk through life with peace in their hearts, Matthew 25:34; 2 Corinthians 5:21?

_____

    b. How are God's people to demonstrate, day by day, that they are sheep following a Heavenly Shepherd, Matthew 25:35,36?

_____

    c. In what way might John 14:7–27 be understood as a summary of Units 1–5?

_____

More SUPPLEMENTARY HELPS

A Modern Mary Sits at Jesus' Feet

Luke 10:38–42 describes Mary sitting at Jesus' feet to be taught by Him. The following conversation between Jesus and a present-day Mary can be read as a personal devotion, or used as a "dialog sermon" during worship. If it is used as a dialog sermon, using a female and male reader, perhaps the male presence could be an invisible one with only his voice being heard on an audio system. If the suggested conversation is seen as a little too long to be used this way, the first two pages might be omitted, with the dialog beginning after the break line included in the script.

Mary: Jesus, it is so kind of You to spend time with me.

Jesus: Mary, you are My sister. How can I help you?

Mary: I want to talk with You about my prayer life.

Jesus: I will be delighted to talk with you about that. Where shall we begin?

Mary: Jesus, I usually pray silently—in my thoughts. But I find that my prayer thoughts are rather blurry. They go here and there and everywhere—and disappear. How can I improve my prayer life?

Jesus: I suggest this: Go alone into a room or to some quiet spot, and either pray out loud, or whisper the words and sentences very quietly. Doing that will really help you focus more on what you say to Me.

Think about how your parents taught you to speak when you were a child. They taught you one or two words—then a few more words—and then helped you put words together to make a sentence. Practice doing that—first by yourself, then within your family circle, and then with your friends. My desire is that My brothers and sisters work at helping each other pray in a meaningful way—My way.

Mary: I hear You saying that I should practice praying?

Jesus: Indeed, I am! My brothers and sisters need to do that. Think about people who have become famous as sports figures. Tennis players, golfers, swimmers, and athletes practice for months and years before they eventually perform in public. When My brothers and sisters practice praying for months and years, it is amazing how well they learn to pray—and how they can help others learn to pray.

Mary: Jesus, the Gospels tell us that when You prayed, You'd go alone to some lonely place. Why?

Jesus: When I prayed, I never sought the approval of others. I sought only the approval of My Father in heaven. I want My brothers and sisters to pray to develop discipleship—not to display their skill with words. I never prayed to inform My Father of anything. I prayed only that I might know His way, and walk in His way.

Mary: Jesus, I have friends who are seriously ill. They tell me that they pray to be healed—but they don't get healed.

Jesus: I know that it can be very difficult for people to face up to the fact that they are seriously ill, and might never get well again. But My Father can use people's sickness in wonderful ways. He can teach them what they really need to know—that they are mortal, and will eventually die. All people need to prepare for their eventual death, and take seriously what I have done for them, and what I want to do for them when they leave this world.

When one of your friends is sick, remember that you can serve that person—and when you serve that person, not only are you acting on My behalf, but you are also really serving Me.

Mary: But how am I to understand things if I myself get very sick?

Jesus: Well, think of it this way. You are either a healthy Jesus serving a Jesus in need, or you are a Jesus in need giving others the opportunity to serve Me through serving you.

Mary: Sometimes I feel that I know so little about what Your Father is really like.

Jesus: My Father has revealed so much about His heart and character in the story that runs through the Bible—from cover to cover. Moreover, look at what I am like and you see what My Father is like.

Mary: How do I talk with God in prayer—when I cannot hear anything that He says to me.

Jesus: My Father talks to you through the Bible, His written Word. And above all, He talks to you through Me—His Living Word. When you read and study His Word and My life, My Father and I send the Holy Spirit to help you understand, believe, and live out what you read, see, and learn.

Mary: Why should I tell God my needs when He already knows all about them?

Jesus: My Father knows all about your needs—you are right. But He wants to help you think through the difference between needs and greeds. His concern is not that you might possess more, but that you might learn to become more and more like Me, your Brother.

Mary: Some of my friends tell me that they prayed to God to bless them—and He did, for they have become quite wealthy. I have often prayed to be blessed, but I am anything but wealthy—even though I prayed in Your name, Jesus. What am I to think about all this?

Jesus: First, some people think of being blessed in terms of how wealthy they become and what material goods they accumulate. I taught My disciples that being blessed has nothing to do with what they possess; it has only to do with whom they reflect—Me.

And—to pray in My name is not some magic formula to ensure that you will get what you ask for. It means that you want to pray as I prayed. Your want your life to reflect My life—as much as possible.

Mary: Jesus, although the Gospels tell us that You went aside to pray, they tell us very little what You prayed about. Why?

Jesus: The more you learn about how I lived, the more you understand what I prayed about. I only prayed that I might know My Father's will, and do it—no matter what that might mean for Me.

Mary: You taught that we should pray constantly. But we are busy people.

Jesus: Yes, I want my people to pray constantly—but that does not mean they are to spend life on their knees. Not at all. I want My people to understand that I walk beside them every second of every minute of every day. And I want them to talk with Me constantly about how I think they should speak, and think, and act.

Mary: Jesus, I'd like You to help me understand the guidelines for prayer You shared with Your disciples.

Jesus: Not only with My disciples, but with all My brothers and sisters. And you are one of My sisters.

Mary: Jesus, although You sometimes prayed all night, the Bible does not tell us what You prayed about.

Jesus: The more you understand what I taught and how I lived, the more you understand what I prayed about.

Mary: The suggested prayer You gave Your disciples is quite short.

Jesus: I taught My disciples a short prayer with a big meaning.

Mary: Jesus, You said we could begin our prayers with:
> *Our Father in Heaven.*

Jesus: I did. What questions do you have about those words?

Mary: Several. To begin with, when I pray, I usually pray alone, so why should I pray in the plural?

Jesus: Mary, you belong to a large world-wide family of My brothers and sisters. I want you to pray not only for yourself, but also for all the other members of My family. I want you to devote life to becoming more like Me, but I also want you to help others do the same.

Mary: It amazes me that You say I can address God the way You did—as "Father," as "Daddy."

Jesus: Remember, when I prayed in the Garden during the night before I was nailed to a cross, I addressed My Father as "*Abba*, Father," or "*Daddy*, Father." I lived, and died, and rose again to make it possible for My brothers and sisters to do the same.

Mary: Would You please explain a little more what doing that might mean for me?

Jesus: Just as children can talk to their earthly father at any hour of the day and night, you can talk with My Father who is your Father at any hour of the day or night.

Mary: I am a little puzzled, then, about our Father being "in Heaven." Those words suggest He is a long way away—somewhere up in the sky.

Jesus: Mary, those words do not mean that our Father is *distant*. They mean that He is *different*. When you pray to our Father, you are not sending words into outer space. You are talking to our Father who is beside you and around you all the time.

Mary: What else should I think about when speaking to our Father as "Daddy"?

Jesus: My Father is never moody. He is never tired. He knows what is best for you. He can and will do what is best for you.

Mary: That is so comforting!

Jesus: Indeed it is. In that part of the world where I carried out My ministry, when children addressed their father as "daddy," they knew that he was close to them, that he had authority over them, and that he provided them with security in life. The same applies to *My* Father and *your* Father.

Mary: That is very reassuring.

Jesus: There is yet more, Mary. When children grow up in a home on earth, they know that the home belongs to their father. I want My brothers and sisters to understand that our Father made and owns everything—the universe, the ground on which you walk, the body in which you live, the house in which you reside. My Father makes possible your every heartbeat, your every breath. He is *lending* you life, and *sustaining* your life.

Mary: I really need to think a lot about that. But, Jesus, I've got many more questions.
>   *Hallowed be Your <u>name</u>.*

Does that mean that I am to be careful about how I say words like "Father, Daddy"?

Jesus: When I walked around on this planet several thousands years ago, many people felt that My Father was too holy and too awesome to address as "God," so they used terms that *referred* to "God" without *saying* God. Terms like "Thy name." But remember what I told you a little earlier? You are invited to address our Father as "Daddy."

Mary: I certainly will always remember that. But please tell me a little more about the word "hallowed."

Jesus: Mary, always remember: My Father's concern is never His ego. It is always your happiness—and the happiness of all people.

Mary: So "hallowed" means more than just saying "Father, Daddy" the right way?

Jesus: Certainly. Mary, let's jump forward to, "on earth as it is in heaven." Those words apply to the first three prayer statements I shared with My disciples. Remember them?

>   *Hallowed be Your name—on earth as it is in heaven;*
>   *Your kingdom come—on earth as it is in heaven;*
>   *Your will be done—on earth as it is in heaven.*

Mary: Yes, I remember them. But, Jesus, please help me understand what "on earth as it is in heaven" implies.

Jesus: In My Father's presence, all *is well*. On earth, all *is not well*.

Mary: I can understand that.

Jesus: When you pray these words, you are saying something like this: "Daddy in heaven, help me to know what You are really like, what You have done for me, and how You want me to live. And help me to inspire others to do the same—so that You might be honored on earth as You are in the world beyond our sight."

Mary: Jesus, You said a minute or so ago that all is well in the presence of Your Father in heaven. Please explain what this means also in relation to those next two petitions.

Jesus: Mary, you know that when I walked around during My earthly ministry, Satan was there the whole time trying to sidetrack Me from walking the way of a servant, and to stop Me from going to the cross. Although I overcame Satan when I went to the cross, he is still around as the world's Number One liar and deceiver. He does not want people to understand Me, to believe in Me, or to follow Me. He wants

people to live for self, self, self. He wants them to ask only, "What's in it for me." I know you are aware of this.

Mary: I am, Jesus. I see that tendency within myself—and in the lives of all around me.

Jesus: Well, the more you understand, the more you see what you are asking in those next two petitions: "Dear Daddy in heaven, when we know Jesus, Your Son, as our forgiving Savior and follow Him as servant Lord, all is well. Your kingdom has come. But Satan is still hard at work. He wants to be the king of my life. Help me to see and flee his delusions and lies, and to know and submit to You as King in all I think, say, and do. And use me to inspire others to do the same."

Mary: And the next petition?

Jesus: It continues along the same lines: "Dear Daddy, where we live, Satan's will is done. Help me to see it, and to flee it, and to know and do Your will—as You revealed and taught it through Your Son, Jesus the servant Messiah.. And empower me to help others know and do Your will."

Mary: I am beginning to get it. The light is getting brighter. I am beginning to understand that in these first three petitions, I am not merely asking God to do something for me. I am committing myself to conform to His plan for my life, and to help others to do the same. I certainly have a lot more thinking to do.

Jesus: I am happy to hear you say that. Are you ready to move on to the next petition?

Mary: Yes, I am. Jesus, I have some questions about:
Give us this day our daily bread.

Jesus: I welcome your questions.

Mary: Pardon me being a little frank, but:

Why "give" when I work to get my daily bread?

Why "us" and "our" when *my* concern is that *I* might eat to stay alive?

Why "this day" and "daily" when I probably have many days ahead of me?

Why "bread" when I need many other things as well.

Sorry for all these questions, Jesus!

Jesus: Mary, I'll respond to your list of questions with one of My own. How much do you pay for a loaf of bread?

Mary: I am sure You already know, Jesus. A few dollars, depending on what kind of bread I buy.

Jesus: Mary, you have never paid a penny for a loaf of bread in your life. My Daddy has always given it to you freely.

Mary: I don't get it. I work. I earn money. I hand it over at the check-out every time I buy bread—or anything else.

Jesus: Mary, have you ever created a grain of wheat or rice, or a kernel of corn?

Mary: Well... no!

Jesus: Only My Father can do that. A farmer takes a grain of wheat or rice, or a kernel of corn that My Father makes, and places it into the soil My Father owns. Then My Father sends His rain and His sunshine— and He provides that farmer with perhaps fifty grains. So, when you hand over money at the checkout, you are not paying for the bread. You are paying the farmer for planting and reaping, the trucker for carrying, the miller for grinding, the baker for baking, and the storekeeper for putting it on the shelf. But My Father gives you the bread.

Mary: Oh!

Jesus: Mary, how much did you pay for your house?

Mary: Well, quite a lot, really. I'm sure you already know how much it cost me.

Jesus: When you understand bread as My Father's provision for you, then you see that *He* owns what you refer to as *your* house, *your* car, *your* furniture, and *your* clothes. You have never paid for anything in your life. You have merely handed over some money, some stored service, to those who produce these things, or put them together. *My Father* owns all those things you have been calling *yours*. My Father is merely *lending* them to you.

Mary: Well, I do understand a little bit about that. I pray before every meal.

Jesus: What do you say?

Mary: Well, Jesus, You already know. But, for the record, my family and I say:

Come, Lord Jesus, be our Guest, and let this food to us be blessed.

Jesus: Quite nice—but have you thought about the fact that I do not have to "come" to your table? *I* never come to *your* table; *you* come to *My* table. *I* am never *your* Guest; *you* are always *My* guest.

Mary: Oops—sorry! I guess You are right. Well, can You suggest a better table prayer?

Jesus: Try this one:

Lord, we thank You for
> *the food before us,*
> *the friends beside us,*
> *the love between us, and*
> *Your presence among us.*

Mary: I like that.

Jesus: So do I! It reminds you that I am the one Who sets food before you—with a little cooperation from you, of course. It also reminds you that your family is a community, and that each is to live to love and serve the others within that community. And it reminds you that whatever you do, you do it in My presence and before My eyes..

Mary: Jesus, You are really challenging me to think as never before.

Jesus: Good! When You pray about daily bread, you are saying:

Lord, You are the owner of all things—including what I think of as my body and life.
You provide all the things I use.
I trust You to continue to provide my needs—not my greeds.
Please help me to understand Your provision and care, and to be grateful.
Help me to thank You for what You supply me with today, and
        to trust You to supply my needs tomorrow.
Help me understand that all of us on Planet Earth are to see ourselves as one big family.
Help me to see myself as one called to work toward providing the needs of all people.

Mary: I am going to have to spend the rest of my life thinking all of that out.

Jesus: Not only thinking about it, but living it out. And remember, I'll be walking beside you all the way through life to understand and live out what we have been talking about. My one desire is that you find peace, joy, meaning, and fulfilment in life.

Mary: Thank you so much, Jesus. Your presence means so much to me. But I'd like your help to understand the next petition:

> *Forgive us our sins, as we have already forgiven the sins of others.*

Jesus: Mary, when You ask Me for forgiveness, you are not bringing forgiveness into existence at that moment. You are grasping what has been there all along.

Mary: I think I understand that. But I know that there are big implications to all this.

Jesus: Indeed, there are. I want those who lay claim to the forgiveness I have won for them to forgive others *before* they ask Me to forgive them.

Mary: That seems right and fair—better, heavenly! But I note that You also refer to my sins as my "debts." Why?

Jesus: I made people to live to serve Me and others full-time in all they do. Those who do not do that are not only in debt to others—they are also in debt to Me. They have failed to serve Me by serving others. I want people to be aware of what they have failed to do for Me and others, and to put things right between themselves and Me, and themselves and others.

Mary: Jesus what about those last statements:
>   *Lead us not into temptation,*
>   *but deliver us from the Evil One?*

It almost sounds as though we are asking You not to lead us into tempting situations.

Jesus: Mary, I never lead you into tempting situations. But please always remember that the powers of sin around and within you seek to seduce you into walking *their* way—not *My* way. But whenever you find yourself caught up in the ways of sin, I am always there to rescue you from those ways.

Mary: That is so encouraging.

Jesus: I am happy to hear that you understand. I want you, and all My brothers and sisters, to live together as a caring family, to pray for forgiveness for each other, and to help each other become more and more like Me.

Mary: What about that last statement, "Deliver us from the Evil One?" Many of my friends do not believe there is an Evil One.

Jesus: There *is* an Evil One—and I had to deal with that Evil One throughout My life and ministry. So do you today. The Evil One did not want Me to live the servant life that I lived, and tried to stop Me going to the cross. Still today the Evil One wants you to focus on getting more, and enjoying more. He wants to seduce you into being successful as the world sees success—rather than to be faithful, as My Father and I define being faithful.

Mary: The older I get, the more I understand that the Evil One works through things like entertainment programs and shopping malls to occupy my mind and to misdirect my life.

Jesus: Mary, the Evil One is every spirit, institution, power, and pressure that seeks to sidetrack you from serving *Me* and *others* into serving *yourself*. But remember that I am always beside you to help you detect the Evil One's strategies and tricks—and to empower you to walk My way.

Mary: Jesus, as You know only too well, in our churches today we conclude Your prayer with:
For Yours is the Kingdom, the power, and the glory forever and ever. Amen.

Although I have some ideas about what these words imply, I would like to hear how You would have us understand them.

Jesus: When I carried out My ministry, Caesar thought that he ruled the world, that he alone possessed the power to decide the course of history, and that all should honor him as the most glorious ruler on earth. He dealt brutally with those who opposed him.

My Father wants all people to know Him as the Owner of creation, as the One who has forgiven people their sins, and as the One who wants to gather all people into a caring, sharing family of grateful sons and daughters.

My Father's concern is not His ego, but the happiness of all—forever and ever, throughout this life and the life to come.

Mary: Wonderful! One word to go—"Amen."

Jesus: It does not mean, "The End." It means, "Lord, I commit myself to translate the words I have said with my *lips* into actions in my *life*."

Mary: Jesus, the insights You have shared with me flood my life with meaning and purpose. Please help me grow in my understanding of Your love for me, and of Your will for my life.

Jesus: Mary, dear sister, always remember that I am beside you at all times, and want nothing more than that we continue to talk with each other throughout this present life, and that to come.

Mary: Jesus, thank you so much for speaking with me. I am overawed!

Jesus: And I am delighted!

Suggested Prayers

Praise for Creation

Almighty God:
The heavens declare Your majesty.
The stars reveal Your power.
The earth shows Your wisdom.
The seas proclaim Your might.
We look with wonder at the universe in which we dwell.
We praise You for the ground on which we walk.
We honor You for the body in which we live.
We thank You for Your provision
of food to empower us,
of water to refresh us,
of air to sustain us, and
of the beauties of nature to delight us.
We thank You for assuring us that we live in Your eternal, caring presence.
We praise You that although we cannot see You,
we know who You are,
where You are, and
what You are like.
We glorify You for revealing Yourself to us through Your written Word,
and for showing us Yourself through Your Living Word, Jesus the Messiah.
As we make our pilgrimage through time into eternity,
grant us humility in our mind,
peace in our spirit,
meaning in our life, and
a sure hope in our heart.
Inspire us to live as citizens of Your eternal Kingdom
until we enter Your Eternal Home.
In the Name of Your beloved Son and our precious Brother, Jesus the Messiah. Amen.

For the nations of the world

Almighty God, You have made this world,
You own this world, and
You provide for this world.
Gracious God, in the Person of Jesus You surrendered Yourself to death on a cross, and
conquered the power of death through His resurrection,
so that we might have forgiveness, meaning, peace, and joy.
In all that we do, use us as Your instruments
to point people of all nations to Your way of serving, caring, and sharing.
May our one desire in life be that all people know, trust in, and follow Jesus the Messiah.
We pray in His forgiving, inspiring, empowering name. Amen.

Birth of a child (general)

Lord God, You who form our body and mold our life,
  we thank You for the gift of a child to (parents' names).
We pray that You will preserve in good health the life You have entrusted to their care.
We pray that You will knit together parents and child in bonds of love.
Make them aware of Your goodness to us.
In times of difficulty, strengthen within the parents the spirit of tenderness.
Enable them to minister to their child in kindness, love, and joy.
Inspire them to rejoice in the presence of Jesus within their home,
  and to teach their child to know Him,
    to trust Him, and
      to follow Him.
Grant to us all, whose honor it is to belong to Your eternal family, and
  to have Jesus as our heavenly Brother,
    a godly demeanor and holy habits.
In His loving, forgiving, and eternal name. Amen.

Birth of a child (parents)

Dear heavenly Father, thank You so much for entrusting to us this child.
We praise You for the wonder-filled way You used our bodies to form another life.
Help us always to remember that our child is really Your child.
Empower us to care for her as You want her cared for.
Help us teach her to know Your Son as her Savior, Lord, and Brother,
  and to think, speak, and live as He did.
Inspire us always to show her the Lord we want her to embrace in faith.
As we provide an earthly home for her, equip us to teach her about the Heavenly Home
  You have prepared for all Your sons and daughters.
May we and she remain faithful to You throughout this life
  and one day know the joy of family life
    in Your eternal presence.
In the name of Jesus, our loving and forgiving Brother. Amen.

Birth of a child (grandparents)

Gracious God, we thank You for the children You have brought into our lives.
And now we thank You for the child You have given to our children.
Make us aware of the miracle that we are.
Remind us at all times that You not only made us, but You also continue to own us.
Help us provide support and guidance to our children
  as they seek to raise Your gift Your way.
We thank You for gathering us into Your family on earth,
  and we look forward to being part of Your Eternal Family in Your Eternal Home.
In the name of our heavenly Brother Jesus,
  the Kings of Kings and Lord of Lords. Amen.

sB

For the sick

O God, You are indeed the Giver of every good gift.
Today, we pray for all who are dear to us—and to You.
We ask You to preserve them outwardly in body, and
   inwardly in spirit.
Teach those in pain
   to rejoice in Your forgiving love,
     to trust in Your limitless mercy, and
      to walk in Your wonderful ways.
Use them and us to reveal Your ways and wisdom
   to those who walk in darkness, doubt, and despair.
Grant us peace in knowing that when this life is done,
   true life will begin.
In the name of Jesus the Messiah, He who is Life abundant and eternal. Amen.

Dealing with sickness (parents with sick child)

Lord of heaven and earth,
   we thank You for Your presence and strength.
We ask You this day to help us minister to our sick child
   in a way that will bring honor to You.
Help us to care for her in the spirit of Jesus.
Remind us that in caring for her, we are really serving Jesus.
Remind us at all times that we are not here to live comfortably,
   but in a way that will reflect our faith in Jesus
     as our forgiving Savior and our caring Lord.
In His loving name. Amen.

Dealing with sickness (adult)

Loving heavenly Father, thank You for lending me life.
Thank You for providing for my needs throughout this life,
   and the promise that You will care for me throughout the life to come.
Grant me Your wisdom, power, and patience as I seek to deal with my health problems
   in a way that will do honor to Jesus, my heavenly Brother.
Through my present challenges, teach me that I have here no abiding city,
   and that I am but a pilgrim on my way to Your Eternal City, the Heavenly Jerusalem.
Use me, through my attitudes and actions, to witness to others about Your eternal promises.
In the midst of my pain, empower me to deal with life's difficulties in a way
   that will point others to Jesus' mind and manner.
As Jesus looked beyond the pain of the cross to the victory beyond,
   sustain me in the sure hope that there will come a day
   when my earthly tears will give way to heavenly joy.
I pray in the name of Him who waits to welcome me into His Eternal Home. Amen.

For the distressed

Loving and caring Lord, pour out Your mercy
>*on those lacking in compassion—transform them;*
>*on those deluded in faith—instruct them;*
>*on those with broken hearts—comfort them;*
>*on those struggling with temptation—rescue them;*
>*on those who have fallen from faith—raise them up.*

In all things, O Lord, help us to be
>*Your caring eyes,*
>*Your compassionate heart,*
>*Your serving hands, and*
>*Your witnessing children.*

In Jesus' great and forgiving name. Amen.

Guidance in life

Dear Jesus, our forgiving Savior and servant Lord,
>*You alone are the way, the truth, and the life.*

Lead us, so that we may not stray from Your way.
Guide us, so that we seek nothing but Your truth.
Inspire us, so that we may make known Your life.
Teach us through Your Holy Spirit
>*what to believe,*
>>*what to do, and*
>>>*where to find rest—now and forever.*

In Your precious name. Amen.

For renewed zeal

Merciful Father, we confess that we have done little to make known Your grace and glory.
Forgive us our neglect.
Pardon our shortcomings.
Give us a greater zeal to know and share Your truth.
Make us more diligent in our prayers.
Enlighten us to be more Christlike in our caring and sharing.
Empower us to enlarge the borders of Your kingdom.
Sustain us throughout this life with Your forgiving grace
>*until we enter that Kingdom where we shall see and praise You to all eternity.*

In the name of our eternal and forgiving Brother, Jesus, Your Son and our Messiah. Amen.

For greater consecration

Great and gracious God, during the day that now dawns,
sustain us in all our comings and goings.
Make us aware of Your holy presence around us,
and Your holy purpose for us.
Help us to surrender ourselves to do the work
that You created us to do,
and call us to do.
Guide us to find rest, not in outward delight,
but in inward dedication to Your will for our lives.
May we rejoice in Your peace during our earthly pilgrimage,
and look forward to sharing Your Eternal Day
with the community of those who have gone before us.
In the name of Your eternal, forgiving, caring Son. Amen.

Celebrating a birthday

Eternal Father, the Source of all life,
thank You for forming me as You did, and
for sustaining my life since the day of my birth.
Thank You for using my parents and others to teach me to know You.
Thank You for adopting me into Your family in Holy Baptism,
and for declaring Jesus, Your Son, to be my Eternal Brother.
During whatever moments, days, months, and years You may continue to grant me,
help me keep my eyes fixed on Jesus as the Lord of the life You are lending me.
Through Your Holy Spirit, teach and inspire me to look to Jesus alone
to direct my walk through this world,
to guard my bed as I sleep,
to guide me in moments of confusion,
to deliver me in days of danger,
to defend me against all spiritual enemies,
to comfort me in times of trouble,
to sustain me in times of sickness,
to reassure me when death draws near, and finally
to close my eyes in smiling peace.
Throughout whatever days You continue to lend me,
grant me the joy of knowing that when my eyes close in this world,
Jesus will open them again,
welcome me into His eternal presence where death is no more, and
walk beside me forever.
I praise You for the peace, joy, and hope that are mine in Him. Amen.

Those who teach children

Good Shepherd, You who lead Your sheep and carry Your lambs in Your arms,
grant to all whose joy it is to teach Your lambs
patience,
tenderness,
sincerity,
holy habits, and
loving dispositions.
Empower all teachers, parents, and members of Your flock
a fervent but loving desire to make You known to each other, and
to all who do not know You.
As we, Your sheep, walk through this world, inspire us to ignore its many voices,
and hear and heed only Your voice.
Grant that we, Your sheep and lambs,
who received the sign of Your cross on our foreheads at our Baptism
may follow You with joy until that day comes
when You will tenderly carry us
into Your Eternal Sheepfold.
To You alone be all praise, honor, and glory. Amen.

For an approaching marriage

Lord Jesus, through Your presence at a wedding in Cana in Galilee,
You honored the holy estate of matrimony.
Bless those who are about to receive this Your gift to us and them.
As they walk through life together,
teach them to show their gratitude to You
by giving life to each other.
Empower each to be a source of
companionship in joy,
comfort in sorrow,
strength in need,
wisdom in perplexity, and
hope when life in this world draws to a close.
May they so know and honor Your empowering and forgiving presence
that they may eventually participate in that eternal Marriage Supper
which You have prepared for them and for us in Your Eternal Home.
To You alone be all praise, honor, and thanks. Amen.

For those about to be confirmed

Loving Lord and Savior,
You who prepared Your disciples for the coming of the Comforter, the Holy Spirit,
touch the hearts and minds of those now studying Your Word
in preparation for their day of confirmation.
As they walk through life during the coming years,
make them aware of Your presence,
and of their need to grow in their knowledge of Your grace and will.
Grant that we, who were marked with Your cross on the day of our Baptism,
may embrace that cross fervently within our hearts,
and reflect it with ever greater understanding in our lives.
Make each of us aware of Your presence within and around us,
so that we, who know the honor of sharing Your Holy Meal on earth,
may experience the joy of Your Eternal Banquet in heaven.
To You alone be all praise, honor, and glory. Amen.

Before Holy Communion

Loving Lord and forgiving Savior,
thank You for inviting me to come into Your presence.
Thank You for assuring me that although I come with downcast eyes,
You await my coming with a smile on Your face.
Thank You for assuring me, that
although I have nothing to offer You but the burden of my many sins,
You have everything to offer me.
For You not only forgive me.
You also invite me to share table fellowship with You.
You call me to celebrate my adoption into Your eternal family.
Lord, I come.
Empower me to come in fervent sincerity,
and to depart in joyous humility.
In my coming and in my going,
sustain me in my relationship with You so that I may ever remember that
I am never alone.
You walk beside me.
I pray that, as You walk beside me, You will empower me
to become more and more what You wish me to be.
As You walk beside me, remind me constantly
that the day is coming when You will invite me to take part in Your Eternal Banquet!
I pray that You too will come quickly
so that my joy may be full.
To You who offer so much
to those who have nothing to offer
be all praise and glory! Amen.

After Communion

Holy Father, almighty and everlasting God,
we thank You for the privilege of sharing in Your Holy Meal.
We thank You for lifting from us the burden of sin,
and for filling our hearts with the peace of Your forgiveness.
We praise You for assuring us that the meal we have shared
is but a foretaste of things to come.
As we walk through this world as pilgrims on their way to Your eternal Promised Land,
build around us a fence through which the Evil One cannot pass,
and clothe us with armor which his darts cannot pierce.
Surround and fill us with Your light, love, peace, and calm.
Empower us to do with joy the things that You call us to do
so that Jesus, Your Son, might be known, seen, believed in, and followed
by many who still walk in the ways of darkness, doubt, and despair.
As Jesus gave His life for us, inspire us to dedicate life to Him.
Inspire us through Your grace to offer You our will and our works,
at all times and in all ways.
In the name of Jesus we pray and give thanks. Amen.

A coming vacation

Heavenly Father, in Whom alone we find peace for our heart and spirit,
be with us during the coming days as we seek rest from our daily toil.
Protect us as we travel.
May the power of sin not spoil our enjoyment.
Open our eyes to see the beauties of Your creation.
May the sense of Your presence add to our happiness.
Bless our fellowship and our laughter.
Renew us in heart, body, and mind
so that, upon our return, we may serve You faithfully
in the life to which You have called us.
We offer these prayers to You in whom is all joy and gladness.
And we pray in the name of Him
through Whose victory over sin and death we possess eternal rest. Amen.

sB

For one about to leave home

Eternal, gracious, and caring God,
  we commit to Your care a loved one soon to live in a world of strangers.
Deliver him from the pain of loneliness.
Grant him courage, wisdom, and self-control.
Provide him with right judgment in all things.
May Your light surround him,
  and Your presence strengthen him.
Wherever life may lead, may he find
  a true house of God, and
    a loving family of friends.
Grant him at all times health of body and spirit.
Sustain him and us during the coming separation,
  and remind us that when we pass through the Gate of heaven,
    into the presence of our beloved Brother, Jesus,
      we shall share eternal fellowship with each other,
        and the tears of separation will be no more.
We pray in the name of our crucified and risen Lord
  Who will never leave us or forsake us. Amen.

For those who travel

Gracious God, we pray for those who travel by land, sea, or air.
Grant them a safe journey,
  a quiet time,
    a happy arrival, and
      a joyous return.
May they use whatever silent hours You grant them
  to ponder the joy of Your presence,
    the wonders of Your creation,
      and the treasures of Your eternal truth.
Use whatever travels we undertake to remind us
  that we are all on a pilgrimage through life.
Sustain us with the sure hope that when we arrive at that Final Destination,
  You will be waiting to greet us as our Heavenly Host,
    and to welcome us into Your Heavenly Mansion.
To You, Who alone grants power and peace along the way, be all thanks and praise. Amen.

When feeling lonely

Lord, I am surrounded by so many
but feel so lonely.
Help me to cope.
Open my heart to Your constant presence.
Remind me that You are always beside me as the Friend of sinners.
Help me to look outwardly, not inwardly.
Teach me to ask, not what others should do for me,
but what I should do for others.
Help me to find life by giving it away.
In all things, O Lord, make me aware of the presence of Jesus beside me throughout this life,
and of the certainty of Jesus waiting for me at the Gate of Heaven.
I pray in the name of the Eternal Friend with whom You have provided me. Amen.

To bear witness to others

Almighty and gracious God:
I thank You for teaching me that You made and own all things,
and that You are the Lord of time and eternity.
I praise You for making me a member of Your eternal family
through the life, death, and resurrection of Your Son and my Brother, Jesus the Messiah.
Loving Lord, in this Your world so many are
blind to Your presence,
deaf to Your Word, and
ignorant of Your wisdom.
Plant within me the heart of Jesus.
Guide me in the ways of Jesus.
Enable me to show the presence of Jesus.
Help me to encourage people to lift their eyes
from the deceptions of this material world
to the truths of Your eternal world.
Equip me to deliver people from walking Satan's ways
and to guide them into walking saintly ways.
May my one desire always be
that I might help those around me know true joy now
and eternal joy in the life to come.
I pray in the name of Him whom You have declared the Lord of time and eternity. Amen.

When financially challenged

Caring and compassionate God,
    You have granted me the gift of life, and
        have promised to provide for my needs.
Lord, at this time in my life, grant me Your guidance and wisdom.
Help me to understand why I see myself as financially challenged.
Help me to deal with the dilemma in which I find myself.
Help me to distinguish between needs and greed.
Help me to ignore the call of the world, and
    hear only Your call to discipleship.
Remind me that Your goal for my life is that I live, not comfortably, but usefully.
Equip me to manage my mind and my money
    in a way that reflects the manner of Jesus.
Empower me to understand that I own nothing—neither life nor money.
Teach me that to be blessed has nothing to do with what I possess
    but everything to do with Whom I reflect.
As I walk through this earthly life,
    grant me Your heavenly wisdom to understand that
        Your Son and My Lord became the poorest of the poor
            so that I might be rich in heart, life, and eternal hope.
And remind me that even when I am poor
    You can use me to make others rich—in the faith and family of Jesus the Messiah.
In His glorious and caring name. Amen.

For one enduring serious challenges in health

O Lord, when I look back into the past
    I am reminded that You have lent me many things.
Grant me wisdom to understand Your ways,
    and strength to praise You whatever each day might bring.
Keep me cheerful when life is challenging.
Keep me content when each hour is difficult.
Keep me peaceful when I want to be demanding.
Keep me grateful for what You have done for me,
    and joyous about what You will still do for me.
Bless those who care for me,
    and help me to show You to them.
Remind me that although I cannot extend my hands in service to others
    I can raise my hands in prayer and praise to You.
Inspire me to understand that although I was often busy with things that did not matter,
    I can now direct my mind to things that matter the most.
Make me ever grateful for the eternal healing that is mine in Jesus Your Son,
    and sustain me with the sure hope that eventually You will gather me into Your embrace
        where the pain of this world gives way to the joy of eternal life in Your presence.
I pray in the name of Jesus, the Great Eternal Healer. Amen.

When determining life's calling

Great and all-knowing God,
I thank you for letting me get a good education.
I ask You to help and guide me as I seek employment.
I pray that You will make it possible for me to find a position
where I can use what I have learned to serve others in a meaningful way.
Help me always to remember that what matters is not how much money I make,
but how much I can serve others,
and help them learn to live usefully.
Thank You for teaching me to know Your Son, Jesus, as my forgiving Savior and servant Lord.
Help me at all times to trust in Him,
and to live in a way that reflects my relationship with Him.
In His name. Amen.

Beginning a new job

Great and wise God,
thank You for helping me find employment.
Grant me a happy relationship with my new employer,
and with my fellow-workers.
When difficult situations arise, help me to handle them in a Christ-like way.
When I find joy in what I do, help me to remember to thank You.
Remind me that You are with me at all times.
Please help me to trust in Your Son as my forgiving Savior, and
to follow Him as my Servant Lord.
Keep me faithful to Him throughout life,
and to seek only His honor and glory.
In His name. Amen.

Loss of job

Great and caring God,
please be with me at this difficult time in life.
Help me to trust You to supply my needs.
If I have to live with less,
help me to learn to do that.
Enable me to find a new position
where I will be able to use my knowledge and abilities in a meaningful way.
During the coming days, weeks, and months,
make me aware of Your presence.
When I find a new place of employment,
remind me to give You thanks and praise.
In Jesus' Name. Amen.

For political leaders

Lord of creation and history,
    I pray for leaders around the world.
Help them understand that we humans live on a planet which we did not make and do not own.
Remind them that each of us is the work of Your hands,
    made from the dust on which we walk.
Help them remember that
    You are not interested in the ways in which we divide ourselves,
        by borders, flags, and skin color.
Help all to remember that people are more important than things.
Grant to all in positions of authority
    wisdom of mind,
    kindness in action,
    clearness in thinking, and
    truth in speaking.
When they are tempted to think of themselves as masters,
    help them to bear in mind that we mere mortals are to have only one Master,
        Jesus the Messiah, Your Son, and our Savior and Lord.
In His loving, forgiving, and serving name we pray. Amen.

Difficult marriage relationship

Lord, thank You for being with me at all times.
You know my every need.
You know the way I must walk to find meaning and joy in life.
Be with me at this difficult time in my marriage relationship.
Help me understand Your plan and will for husband and wife.
Help us both to understand our personal faults,
    rather than focus on the other person's faults.
Remind us of what we promised each other on our wedding day.
Teach us that we are not to demand things of one another,
    but to work at serving each other.
Let us remember that You are the source of love itself,
    and that You are the foundation on which this marriage is built.
Make us aware of Your presence in all we do,
    and to seek Your mind and manner at all times.
Help each of us learn to think, speak, and act like Jesus,
    and to help each other become more like Him.
In His loving and forgiving name. Amen.

Forgiving others

Lord, there are days when I find it so hard to forgive others their sins against me.
Remind me of how much You forgive me every day.
Remind me that Your Son sought only to do His best for those
    who sought to do their worst to Him.
Remind me that I am not to treat others as they treat me,
    but as Jesus has treated me.
Help me to focus, not on what those around me are,
    but on what I can help them become.
Lord, You have forgiven me a multitude of sins against You.
Help me to forgive others their few sins against me.
Remind me that I am not to model my life on those around me,
    but on Him who is constantly beside me.
May I find joy in His presence,
    hope in His forgiveness, and
        joy in His guidance. Amen.

For those in prison

Dear Lord, I pray for those who are in prison.
Help them to reflect on Your truth and their lives so that they might find
    joy in Your presence,
    peace in Your forgiveness, and
    hope in Your promises.
Inspire them to use their many lonely hours to study and ponder Your Word, written and Living,
    so that they might experience that true companionship and freedom
        found only in knowing Jesus as Savior and Lord.
Be with their families and friends,
    and sustain and strengthen the bonds of love among them.
Bless those who minister to them,
    that they might do so with compassion and concern.
We pray in the name of Jesus, who gave His life that we might have eternal life. Amen.

For music

Lord, in this world so full of distracting noises, we thank You for music.
Thank You for empowering some on this troubled planet to create music
    which says things words cannot say,
    which fills us with joy,
    which inspires our minds, and
    which soothes our heart.
We thank you for music which moves
    feet to dance,
    faces to smile, and
    hearts to pray.
Grant us the continuing gift of music
    until You call us to join that heavenly choir
        where we will sing Your praises to all eternity.
We pray in the sweet name of Jesus. Amen.

sB

For animals

Great and gracious God,
You have made all things and
love all things.
We thank you for surrounding us with
birds that fly,
animals that walk, and
creatures that swim.
We thank you for those wondrous works of Your hand that provide people
with joy as they walk,
with strength for their work, and
with devotion in their loneliness.
May we always show kindness
to those who have no voice to speak, and
no power to defend themselves.
May we never find joy in killing,
but ever find joy in caring.
Remind us always that animals, birds, and fish are creatures
that Your hands have made,
and for whom Your heart provides.
We pray in the precious name of the eternal Lamb of God. Amen.

General

Dear Lord and Brother, Jesus:
be near us to protect us,
within us to sustain us,
around us to preserve us,
before us to guide us, and
above us to bless us.
Keep us steadfast in faith,
free from sin
and safe from danger.
Grant us Your light to guide us,
Your courage to support us,
and Your love to unite us.
Be with us when we go,
watch over us when we sleep,
and speak with us when we wake.
Be with us in our going out and our coming in,
in our sorrow and in our joy.
And bring us at last to Your Eternal Rest. Amen.

Dear Lord, keep me
  pure in thought,
  temperate in tongue,
  truthful in speech,
  diligent in work,
  faithful in keeping promises,
  generous toward the needy,
  loyal to family and friends,
  humble in Your presence,
  mindful of my mortality,
  sure in hope,
  joyous in Your promises, and
  certain about my eternal destiny.
In Jesus' name. Amen

O Lord:
Guide us while we are awake;
Guard us while we sleep.
Empower us to labor diligently.
Help us to walk in Your light,
  to be guided by Your Spirit,
  to please our invisible, but ever-present Brother.
Deliver us from earthly error,
  from foolish fears,
  from enslaving desires, and
  from worldly ambitions.
Assure us that when You bring our years to an end,
  You will welcome us into Your Eternal Home
    where Jesus awaits us,
      and true joy will never cease.
In His name. Amen.

Lord, grant me
>*the serenity to accept the things I cannot change;*
>*courage to change the things I can;*
>*and wisdom to know the difference.*

Living one day at a time;
Enjoying one moment at a time;
Accepting hardships as the pathway to peace;
Taking, as He did, this sinful world as it is,
>*not as I would have it;*

Trusting that He will make all things right
>*if I surrender to His will;*

That I may be reasonably happy in this life
>*and supremely happy with Him forever in the next.*

Amen.   (Reinhold Niebhur)

Day by day, dear Lord, of Thee three things I pray:
to see Thee more clearly,
to love Thee more dearly, and
to follow Thee more nearly
day by day.   (Richard of Chichester)

Prayer does not change God; it changes those who pray.   (Soren Kierkegaard)

Prayer is to be our steering wheel—not our spare tire.   (an adaptation of a statement by
Corrie Ten Boom)

To be a Christian without prayer is no more possible than to be alive without breathing.
(Martin Luther)

He who prays as he ought will endeavor to live as he prays.   (John Owen, Puritan theologian)

*Work as if everything depended upon your work, and pray as if everything depended upon your
prayer.*   (William Booth, founder of the Salvation Army)

Prayer is the gymnasium of the soul.   (Samuel Zwemer, missionary to Islam)

God is not a cosmic bell-boy.   (Harry Emerson Fosdick)

■ We are not to treat God like a waiter whose sole role is to note and deliver our daily order.

■ We do not pray to pressure God for more provisions. We pray that God might pressure us for His
purposes.

■ When we offer prayers to the God above us, we commit ourselves to offer actions to those around us.

- When we pray, we do not hand over responsibilities. Rather, we assume responsibility for doing what we prayed about.

- We do not pray to get what we want; we pray to get what God knows we need.

- "Your Kingdom come" and "Your will be done" are not reminders to God. They are statements of responsibility on the part of those who pray them.

- We pray, not to get material blessings, but to discern God's will. Those who know and do God's will are blessed.

- In prayer, we do not ask God to notice the good we have done. We ask Him to forgive the wrong we have done, and to empower us to become what He wants us to be.

- When God calls us, He bids us to die to the ways of the world and learn to live His way.

- The only way to do away with enemies is to love and serve them into friendship.

- We pray, not so that life in heaven will be as it is on earth, but so that life on earth might become more like it will be in heaven.

- We are to pray, not for a bigger bank balance, but for better relationships.

- We pray, not to be the wealthiest nation in the world, but the wisest.

- As God's saints, we are not people who are no longer tempted. We are those who are learning how to deal with temptation.

- "Amen" means "So be it"—a commitment to do what has been prayed.

- "Amen" signifies the end of *saying*, and the beginning of *doing*.

- As the bride of Christ, God's people pray to do only what pleases the Groom.

- God calls us to put Him not *first*, but *only*.

- Christianity is not the most important *part* of life. It is *all* of life.

- We are not merely to *go* to church. We are to *be* God's church.

- The words, "in Jesus' name," are not a prayer mantra. They are a commitment to embrace Jesus' mind, mission, and manner of life.

■ God does not always remove thorns, but He empowers people to cope with them.

■ Bearing a cross in life can craft character for life.

■ In giving us His prayer, Jesus did not give us a "quick fix" for life's many problems, but guidelines for having a life-long relationship with Him even in the midst of our problems.

■ When we pray to God in heaven, it is important that we see ourselves as living in occupied territory—with Satan as the occupying power.

■ We pray to God, not that we might delight in more dollars, but that we might deal with the devil.

■ We pray, not that we might sit on a throne, but that Jesus might be enthroned in our life.

■ When we pray, our concern must be *necessities*—not *niceties*.

■ We pray, not to live *long*, but to live *lovingly*.

■ We pray, not to put up with people, but to forgive, serve, and disciple them.

■ We pray for the ability to indulge in radical inward self-examination so that we might go forth in radical outward action.

■ We do not pray to *inform* God. We pray that God might *reform* us.

■ God does not need our instruction. We need God's direction.

■ What Jesus taught, Jesus modeled. We are to model what Jesus taught.

■ We are not to seek the roaring approval of the crowds, but the quiet approval of God.

■ We pray, not to collect provisions, but to conform to God's purposes.

■ When we pray from our heart, God understands our language—however stumbling it might be.

■ In prayer, we should thank God for what we have received, rather than remind Him about what we would like to receive.

■ Sports figures practice for years in private what they perform for mere moments in public.

■ How can I say that I am in love with God when I never talk with God?

- The world is God's gymnasium for "working-out" to develop a more Christ-like spiritual fitness.

- God calls us to talk, not merely *about* Him, but *with* Him.

- Prayer is human weakness leaning on divine omnipotence.

- In praying, we are to focus more on a change of character than a change of circumstances.

- We do not pray to impose our will on God, but to submit to God's will for us.

- God answers every prayer—not necessarily *our* way, but certainly *His* way.

- In Jesus' parable of the Pharisee and the publican, the Pharisee bragged, the publican prayed. (Luke 18:9–14).

- The more we understand that it cost Jesus His life to establish His Father's kingdom, the more we wonder why some, who profess to be His followers, are grabbers rather than givers.

- All too often, much wealth finishes up in the pockets of those who preach and promote prosperity.

- The focus of God's people dare not be how much they spend on buildings in which to sit, but on how they might devote life to bringing blessings to others.

- What matters is not having a new church carpet on which to walk with our feet, so much as knowing that we provided a roof over the heads of the homeless.

- Jesus warned against many things, but gave only money divine status as a rival god, Matthew 6:24.

- Do we own our possessions, or do they own us?

- Often those who have the most are aware of the least, and those who have the least are aware of the most.

- Christmas has been made into the biggest commercial event of the year. People spend more time in the cathedrals of commerce than in the community of Christ.

- To separate Holy Communion from washing the feet of others is to tear apart what Jesus bound together.

- If we offer 12-step programs for alcoholics, we should also offer 12-step programs for the greedy (and a host of other common sins).

- Money is a wonderful servant, but a terrible master.

- TV shows us a few of the needs around the world, and then seduces us with commercials designed to persuade us to buy what we do not need, with money we do not have, to impress people who do not care.

- Our goal in life must not be concern for profit, but concern for people.

- There is no such thing as private Christianity. Either Christianity destroys the privacy, or the privacy destroys Christianity.

- When a butterfly flaps its wings in China, it affects the weather patterns around the planet.

- The "supreme sacrifice" is not to die for one's country, but to die to the ways of the world.